Introduction & Author's Note

The discovery of Alianore Audley's Chronicle caused a major stir in academic circles. It threw a new light on the life and times of Richard III, providing answers to a number of previously unresolved questions.

Certain cynical individuals have expressed doubt about the reliability of the Chronicle. However, comparison with other known sources bears out the great bulk of Alianore's narrative. This is as much as can be said for the Croyland Chronicle, the generally accepted work of authority on the period. Even so unlikely an incident as the capture of Gloucester's banner by Lord Stanley is recorded in an old ballad. (See *Richard III as Duke of Gloucester and King of England*, C. A. Halstead, volume 2, p. 67, note 3.)

I have updated some of Alianore's spellings for the modern reader, and ironed out some of her medieval idioms. Apart from this, the text is exactly as she left it.

Brian Wainwright

D1509591

About The Author

Brian Wainwright has had a deep interest in the middle ages for most of his life. He cannot explain this satisfactorily, although he spent a fair bit of his childhood climbing over castles in Wales.

In his teens he developed a particular fascination with the era of Richard II, another king he believes history has sadly misjudged. There were few novels about that period and Brian eventually came across *The White Boar* by Marian Palmer, which started him off on his fascination with the Third Richard. The 14th and 15th centuries remain his favourites and his particular interest is the House of York throughout its existence.

Brian destroyed much of his early writing work due to his dissatisfaction with it, although there are a number of articles in various obscure places. He wrote *The Adventures of Alianore Audley* by way of light relief during a lull in the long task of researching and writing about Constance of York (daughter of the first Duke, Edmund of Langley) in *Within the Fetterlock,* a novel published by Trivium in the USA in 2004.

Brian lives in the North West of England and is currently working on another book about the House of York, centring on Richard III, Francis Lovel and the Mowbray family.

Also by Brian Wainwright:
Within the Fetterlock (ISBN: 0-9722091-1-5)
Trivium Publishing, 2004 (http://www.triviumpublishing.com)

For Christine Wainwright

A wonderful romp set in 15th-century England. The machinations of the Wars of the Roses and life at the court of Richard III are seen through the eyes of royal spy Alianore Audley. Told with zest, a deep love and knowledge of the period, not to say a wicked sense of humour and plenty of tongue in cheek, Brian Wainwright deserves far greater recognition than he currently gets.

Elizabeth Chadwick's Top 10 Historical Novels, *The Guardian*

…Wainwright's *Alianore Audley* holds a place in my heart. What an endearing heroine, if ever there was one. Alianore, by pure mischance (or perhaps great good fortune), leaves her quiet, boring existence in the convent that her brothers have summarily dumped her in. (Where else can a girl in 15th century England go?) Clearly, Alianore is not meant for the contemplative life. The alternative is natural: she becomes a spy for her cousin, Edward IV. Natural? It does seem that way as events unfold. Despite the fact that Alianore is initially sent to the North to gather intelligence for Edward so that she is prevented from getting into mischief, she becomes an invaluable asset to the Yorkist cause.

Alianore's riotously funny insights into the obnoxious and abusive Warwicks, tongue-in-cheek barbs at Margaret Beaufort and Lord Stanley, disrespectful comments about everyone from "Cousin Edward" to the "Tudor Slimebag" (Henry VII), and loving remembrances of Richard and Anne liberally pepper this all-too-brief book. Wainwright has a feel for the period and presents it in a unique and enjoyable fashion.

How to give you who read this review a flavor of the times as seen through Alianore's wickedly funny but loving perspective is tantamount to impossible. You've just got to be there. Read it.

Ilysa Magnus, *The Historical Novels Review*

The Adventures of
Alianore Audley

I

I was ten years old in the 34th year of Mad King Harry the Sixth when Lady Tegolin came to my father at his castle of Newport and asked if she could take me as her pupil.

My father put down his cup of wine and belched. It was the Feast of Corpus Christi, and he was feeling expansive.

"What do you think, my dear?" he asked my mother.

"Mmmm …" grunted Lady Audley, petting one of her one hundred and thirty-two assorted dogs. My mother had but one claim to fame. She was the only woman in the history of England to be kicked out of a convent because of the nuisance caused by her pets. We had no such easy remedy, but after a time you got used to taking care where you put your feet.

"It would be useful to have a poisoner in the family," my brother Edmund declared. "For emergency use only, of course."

Edmund always was the scholarly one among us. He spent years at university, honing his keen sense of morality. I always knew that he would end up as a Bishop. The obnoxious Tudor Slimebag, known to his friends as Our Sovereign Lord King Henry the Seventh, has recently promoted him to the See of Hereford. I'm sure they're very happy with each other.

"I can teach her much more than that," Tegolin snorted.

"I'm sure you can," said my father, "but what is it that interests you in Alianore? Why did you never ask for one of her sisters?"

"She is a Special Child. I have seen her destiny."

"Oh, yes? And how long for her to learn your skills?"

"Seven years for the full course –"

"Seven years? Are you stark, staring mad, woman?"

13

"But I can probably get her through the Preliminary Certificate in just one year. Eighteen months at the most."

"Hmmm," said my father, "and at what cost?"

"The cancellation of my arrears of feudal dues. That's all."

My father got his abacus out and flicked the beads about as he considered the bargain.

"I've heard about you people," he said, frowning, "and some of the things you get up to at night. If I agree to this, I want my child back in good, marketable condition. *Virgo Intacta* and all that. Understood? If one hair of her head is harmed, Lady Tegolin, I shall see to it that little bits of you are stuck up on every gallows from here to Newcastle. And I don't mean Newcastle Emlyn, or the Newcastle near Clun in the Marches, or even Newcastle-under-Lyme. I mean Newcastle-on-Tyne. We have a short way with witches hereabouts."

It sounded a rather long way to me.

"My Lord Audley," Tegolin answered, "I am, above all, a Welsh gentlewoman. Your daughter will be entirely safe in my care. However, I should like to observe that witchcraft is an offence punishable in the ecclesiastical courts, not under temporal jurisdiction. The Bishop of St David's and his Chancellor happen to be among my closest friends, and would be unlikely to proceed against me on the basis of idle rumour. Moreover, contrary to the common perception, witchcraft is not, in itself, a capital crime. I have to say, therefore, that on balance your threats tend to leave me somewhat unmoved."

To my surprise my father laughed at her. "You are in my private Lordship of Cemaes, where I have power of life and death over every man, woman and sheep. On top of that, I am the Chamberlain of South Wales, King Henry's most senior officer in a hundred miles. Believe me, if you give me any hassle you will rapidly be converted into dead meat. Legal niceties won't save you, and as for the Bishop and his Chancellor, they can each have a cheek of my arse to kiss. Now, take the maid, teach her what she needs to know, and bring her back to me undamaged. Or else. Oh, and by the way, I don't want her to learn anything really wicked, like how to stop herself from having babies. Is that quite clear?"

"Absolutely, my lord," said Tegolin. She curtsied, not very deeply, and held out her hand to me.

You will notice that no one had consulted me on the proposal. I was used to this sort of treatment. I was the youngest child of a large family, right at the bottom of the pecking order. I just got told what to do.

Lady Tegolin appeared ancient to me, although I don't suppose that she was more than forty. She was small and dark and round, like many Welshwomen, quite handsome, with a twinkle in her eye that drew men to her. She took me home to her manor house. Do not be impressed by this term. It was built of stone, but the masons had obviously been drunk, lazy, and short of materials. It was one step up from a ruin. No Kentish yeoman would have dared to bring a new wife home to such an abominable pit.

(By the way, I'm not sure how Lady Tegolin came by her title. Her late husband was never knighted, and she was most certainly not the daughter of an earl, marquis, or duke. Those of you who are pedantic will have to come up with your own explanation.)

Tegolin worked on me for months. She read me all the Welsh legends, translating them into English as she went along. Boy, those legends are really something. How anyone with more than a pea for a brain can believe a word of them I shall never know. Maidens emerging from lakes. Giants walking across the sea from Ireland. I ask you!

Then there was the Welsh poetry, beautiful to the ear until it was converted into understandable form, when it almost invariably turned out to be a dirge predicting that Owain Glyndwr would return and drive us out of Wales. Sure thing, Tegolin.

She showed me the herbs to mix if I wanted to force fleas out of my mattress, or if I needed to get a wine stain out of a velvet gown. Things were looking up. This was interesting. Unfortunately, it didn't last, and she was soon rattling on again about how I could become a great lady, the mother of a long line of kings, and so on and so forth.

One night, as we sat by the fire, she asked me what I could see in it.

"Sticks burning. Smoke. Flames. Ash," I said.

"Is that all?"

"Yes."

"You disappoint me, Alianore. I saw your face in Gwenllian's Pool on St Bride's Eve. You are a Special Child. You can have great power. To predict the future. To control events. To have any man you choose. You possess the key to unimaginable wealth. You are linked in destiny with the greatest in the land. Why do you fight it?"

"The concepts you put forward are lacking in intellectual rigour," I said. "I conclude, therefore, that they're just a big pile of crap. I am not a Special Child. What's more, I've no wish to be a Special Child. My desire in life is to be married to a decent gentleman of coat armour, and to bear his sons and daughters. To gossip with my neighbours, to disagree with them about the correct height and angle of a hennin, and to influence the selection of the County Sheriff. In other words, to be ordinary. That, Lady Tegolin, will do me."

"Really, child, you do try my patience! How on earth do you expect to be taken seriously as the heroine of a story, especially one set partly in Wales, unless you understand at least the rudiments of sorcery and have some basic ability to foretell the future? A woman without special powers is merely a chattel. Of no interest to anyone."

"I disagree. Given special powers, anyone can do anything. It takes away all the merit of achievement. It's like King Arthur's magic sword. As long as he wielded it, no one could defeat him. Well, that means that the virtue was in the sword, not in him. Even I could be a great knight with a sword like that. I'd be much more impressed by Arthur if he'd fought his battles with an ordinary sword, and still won them."

"You are a true Saxon," she sighed, "entirely lacking in imagination. Have you no Welsh blood at all? If only you could overcome the handicap! I can see your power. It glows around you. Do you not feel it?"

"I feel a draught from the door," I said. "Are there no competent joiners in Wales? It would certainly be a good idea for you to employ one of them."

She shook her head, despairing of me. "We are going upon an important journey. To Pembroke. I wish to show you the future. England's future."

"You cannot. No one can see the future. It hasn't happened yet. We're making it up as we go along, all of us, like a great big piece of embroidery without a pattern. We've each got a needle. Some of us put in the odd stitch. Others put in a row or two. But no one can say what it'll be when it's all finished."

"You can," said Tegolin, "if you stand back far enough."

The next morning we set out for Pembroke, riding on two stocky, sure-footed little ponies, of the sort that pass for horses in Wales. (Most Welsh people have never seen a real horse, and if they came across one would probably take it to be a dragon or something.) Our only escort was a sturdy boy from Tegolin's stables, who followed us on foot, a spear over his shoulder.

After about ten miles we caught sight of a column of armed men travelling in the opposite direction. It seemed to me that it would be a very good idea to avoid these gentlemen, and the nearer they came the more certain I was that I was right. The wars of York and Lancaster had already kicked off at the time of which I write, and South West Wales was not exactly the place to go for a rest cure.

Tegolin did not seem to be worried. She rode on as if we were running into a party of Observant Friars.

The leader of the cut-throats greeted her politely. (He spoke in Welsh, so I cannot give you his exact words, but the tone was polite.) Tegolin answered him in the same language, and in the same tone, and made him laugh. He touched his helmet and passed on, his nasty band of thugs following him without so much as a glance in our direction.

"You know him?" I asked.

She smiled. "He's Thomas ap Gruffydd. A friend. He's been known to share my bed from time to time, when I've had nothing better in my larder."

"Is he a Yorkist?"

My father had said that the Yorkists were villainous thieves. Thomas ap Gruffydd certainly answered the general description.

"He's on his way to steal someone's property, child. He may do it in the name of the Duke of York. Or in the name of our blessed King Harry and Queen Margaret. Either way, the profit will be his. A useful friend. A bad enemy. Fortunately, he is at the very least as afraid of me as you are of him."

"Because he thinks you are a witch?"

"Because he knows I am. And my power is nothing to what yours could be, if you were but willing to learn the art. You could strike such terror into a man like Thomas ap Gruffydd that he'd have to spend the rest of his natural life sitting on a privy."

"To be feared is to be hated. I'd much rather be loved."

"You can have the love of any man you wish."

"By compulsion? That isn't love. Love comes naturally, or not at all. It cannot be commanded by spells and potions. All you offer me is power, and power is poison. I reject it. I wish to go home."

"You must first come to Pembroke."

"Why? What's happening at Pembroke that's so damned special?"

"A lying-in."

I sighed. Tegolin was, among other things, a skilled and popular midwife. She had taken me to help her bring several children into the world. The first experience of this kind had been interesting, I'll grant you that. But once you've seen one baby born, brother, you've seen them all. They can all be guaranteed to emerge from the same place, naked, bloody and ugly. A king's son gets wrapped up in a better class of cloth, but in all the essentials it's no different whether you're delivering the child of a queen or a goose-girl.

We arrived at Pembroke not long after Christmas. They were still keeping open castle, but the celebrations were muted by the recent loss of their lord's brother, Edmund Tudor, Earl of Richmond, who had been sore wounded at the hands of the Yorkists, and died in captivity at Carmarthen. His lady lay upstairs in the solar, struggling with her swollen belly as she considered the written offers of marriage that were already flooding in. She was a great heiress.

I was surprised to find that the Lady Margaret was not much older than myself. Certainly not above fourteen at the very most. She was extremely small and delicate, and, as heiresses go, remarkably good looking. She was learned, too. Even more learned than my brother Edmund. Her idea of fun was to work her way through a thousand pages of Latin text.

I had my doubts about Lady Margaret Beaufort from the first.

Tegolin was known for her skills even in Pembroke, and we were more than welcome. So it chanced that I was present at the birth of the obnoxious Henry Tudor. If I'd known then what I know now, I'd have taken the opportunity to drop him straight down the shaft of the garderobe.

Lady Margaret was delighted with him, naturally enough. So was Tegolin. She went off into a rambling rhapsody in Welsh. She stopped only when she realised that Lady Margaret had no more idea of what she was saying than I did.

"This child will be our King. Wales shall rule England," she explained.

I could tell that Margaret did not wholly believe this, but the idea still pleased her. She thanked Tegolin in the polite, patronising style that every English lady uses when she receives a posy of flowers from a peasant child.

The women had cleaned up the baby, and were passing him round, satisfying themselves that he had all his bits and pieces. At length one of them handed him to me.

"Ugly little bastard, isn't he?" I said.

I've no idea why I chose these particular words. Or why I spoke so loudly. It may be that I did possess prophetic powers after all.

Lady Margaret sat up in bed, furious. "Get her out of here!" she yelled. "Out, out, out!"

Tegolin was not pleased with me. She scarcely said a word all the way home. That was not at all like Tegolin.

"Wales cannot even rule itself," I said scornfully, trying to get her going again. "It couldn't rule England long enough for an egg to be boiled hard. How could you have come out with such tripe? No wonder Lady Margaret was annoyed. You forget that she's English too. Her father was the Duke of Somerset, not Owain Glyndwr. And Glyndwr's not going to return, either. He was born about 1360, so he'd be nearly a hundred now if he was still alive, which he isn't. If you stopped living in dreams, Tegolin, and got your bloody door fixed, you'd be a lot better off."

She stared at me, long and hard. "You will see, child," she answered. "You will see."

I must admit that my recollection of these events is somewhat hazy. In fact, there are times when I wonder if they happened at all, or whether they are just recollections from some elaborate dream. Even my own dialogue, as I recall it, seems unlikely when you understand that I was only ten or eleven years old. But it is as I recall it.

My brother Edmund tells me that we were never at Newport. That neither one of us, to his certain knowledge, ever set foot in my father's Lordship of Cemaes. That we were brought up entirely in Shropshire at the Red Castle, or Hawkstone as it is sometimes known. That, on a scale of one to ten, the likelihood of my father farming me out to a witch would score about minus seventeen. That he himself, while still a child, a future man of the cloth, would scarcely have suggested that we needed a poisoner in the family.

So where do the memories come from?

I draw to your attention the fact that Edmund is employed by a certain Henry Tudor who is allegedly a king. For him, therefore, lying is a way of life. Part of his job description. History is constantly being rewritten. Today's fact is tomorrow's doubt, and the next day's ludicrous falsehood. You must make your own mind up about the truth.

It is acceptable, I believe, for a story to have alternative endings. I shall go further, and have an alternative beginning. This means that you can ignore everything I have written up to this point. Or not, as you choose.

I was thirteen years old in the 37th year of Mad King Harry the Sixth, when my father was foolish enough to get himself killed while leading the Lancastrian forces at the Battle of Blore Heath.

Queen Margaret of Anjou had been riding around Cheshire and Shropshire with her little son, Prince Edward, handing out the

Prince's badge, a swan, to all and sundry as she tried to build up an army big enough to tackle the Duke of York.

They made a fair sight, the beautiful French Queen and her sweet angel of a Prince. You could see all the men going weak at the knees at the prospect of dying for them. They cheered, and waved their swords in the air, and swore to risk the last drops of their blood. It was enough to make any sensible person throw up.

My father was sixty-one years old. In my opinion he should have made this his excuse and stayed at home by the fire. He probably would have done if it hadn't been for Margaret of Anjou. She flashed her big, blue eyes at him – to say nothing of her big, white breasts – and asked him to take command. I can still see him now, kneeling, with tears flowing down his cheeks, as he thanked her for the honour.

We were at the Red Castle, just south of Whitchurch, not far from the border between Shropshire and Cheshire. It was always my father's favourite home. (The castle is built of red sandstone, hence its name, which is not so much romantic as unimaginative.) Knights and squires from miles around flocked to join us, and clustered around the big map my father had laid out on one of the tables in the hall. They pushed bits of wood around on it, and grunted, and spilled their wine, and agreed that we were going to grind the Yorkists into the dust.

Second-in-command was Thomas, Lord Stanley, a young man then, although you could already see the mean little lines around his mouth. He suggested that his two thousand followers should form a strategic reserve, and place themselves so as to cut off the enemy's retreat.

Stanley was a big cheese, and my father didn't have much choice but to agree to this. He had plenty of men even without Stanley. From the information that was coming in he reckoned that he'd outnumber the Yorkist Earl of Salisbury and his followers by at least two to one.

(He also knew that Sir William Stanley, Lord Stanley's brother, was with the enemy. And that Salisbury was Lord Stanley's father-in-law. Too many Stanley liveries out on the battlefield might have caused confusion.)

They rode out to meet the Yorkists, lambs to the slaughter. I remember my half-sister, Margaret, tying a favour around the arm of her husband, Sir Thomas Dutton. Their son, Peter, no more than seventeen, was honoured in the same way by his betrothed, Alicia Legh. Poor fools, they must have thought that they were going off to some stupid joust.

They were cut to pieces.

Whenever I hear some stupid sprig telling everyone that he longs to prove his manhood in battle I think of young Peter's face that day.

Queen Margaret of Anjou had her horse's shoes replaced back to front, and then made a strategic withdrawal to a prepared position. I don't know where she drew rein, but it was a hell of a way from Blore Heath or the Red Castle. It was many a long year before I set eyes on her again.

II

As far as my brothers were concerned, I was a piece of useless baggage, like a spare bed, and they deposited me in a convent, out of the way, while they got on with the business of killing each other. I say this advisedly, because they didn't all fight on the same side. I had Yorkist brothers and Lancastrian brothers, and they all had a change of coat from time to time. Confusing? You should have tried being me.

Anyway, after a couple of years most of the dust had settled, Daft Harry had been booted from his throne, and we had a new, young King, Edward IV of the House of York. From my point of view very little was happening. Convents are not noted for successions of exciting incidents. However, there was the night when the Bishop's Vicar-General was murdered in the middle of his Visitation.

We found him lying on the grass in the middle of the cloisters. The whole Community gathered round. You could tell that this was going to keep them in gossip for the next century.

"The poor man has obviously had a heart attack," announced the Prioress. "How very unfortunate."

I moved forward to take a closer look. "I think not, Madame," I said. "Look at those marks on the grass. It's quite clear that he's been dragged to his present position. You can also see the mud on the back of his gown."

"That must have happened when he fell," she snorted.

"Except that he fell on his face," I replied, smiling up at her.

I knelt over the body and lifted up his hood. "See, here in his collar. Unless I'm mistaken this is a leaf from the herb commonly known as Lady's Mantle. Found in these precincts only in the herb bed adjacent to the passage leading from your apartments to the cloisters. And here, see, almost lost in the thickest part of his hair. A recent wound. Made, I venture, by a heavy blow from a blunt instrument."

"This proves nothing," said the Prioress, airily. "You are wasting time, child, which could be better devoted to our prayers for this unfortunate man's soul."

"There's one other small piece of evidence, Madame," I continued, standing up again. "You obviously dressed in some degree of haste. No doubt that's why you're wearing his drawers on your head instead of your wimple."

The Prioress ripped off her unsuitable headdress and threw it as far away from her as her strength allowed. Do you know, she was not the least bit amused.

"Take this wretched girl away," she said to the Mistress of Novices. "Whip her well, and lock her up for a month on bread and water. There are far too many unlikely people wandering around solving crimes these days. I am *not* having one in this flaming nunnery!"

I began to worry about my future. The career prospects in convents are pretty limited. And once you've scrubbed one cloister floor, brother, you've scrubbed them all.

The Audley family are an obscure tribe. Few of us have made any mark at all on the pages of history, and if my father had had the wit to stay away from Blore Heath he would have been no exception to this rule. It may surprise you to learn that despite my insignificance I was a close kinswoman of King Edward. In fact, his grandfather and my grandmother were brother and sister, and you don't get much closer to royalty than that without being royal yourself. I saw prospects in this, great prospects. In truth, it seemed to me that we, as a family, had fallen very nicely on our feet. My eldest half-brother, John, now Lord Audley, had changed sides at just the right time, and was now well established in Cousin Edward's favour. Believe me when I say that one Yorkist half-brother on the King's Council is worth a lot more than two Lancastrian full brothers begging their bread in exile.

John was like a second father to me. He was old enough to play the role convincingly, pushing along towards forty. He came to visit me in the convent.

"Hibe dissided to put yew in Lhaddie Wawwick's howse-owd," he said. He had a very bad cold at the time. I thought at first that he was doing a rather poor impression of a Coventry alderman.

"I'd rather go to Court," I said, trying to be persuasive.

"Tuff!" he answered, giving me a brotherly smack across the mouth.

I picked myself up off the floor. "All right, John. You've made your point. Lady Warwick's household it is. Where is she? Not at Warwick, I suppose?"

"Up at Middlumb. Und behabe byourself, or dere'll be twouble."

I don't know what gave him the idea that I wouldn't behave myself. I think he must have been talking to that Prioress. For some reason or other she had taken a real dislike to me.

It only took me about four weeks to get to Middleham, which for those of you who don't know is right at the top end of Yorkshire, and a bit too close to bloody Scotland for comfort. By the time I got there I had the fleas of ten counties climbing all over me, fighting their battles in some very funny places as they argued about who had the right to suck my blood.

Lady Warwick was another of my cousins. (In fact, our mothers were half-sisters. You can paint my quarterings on a shield and they look good enough to go on anyone's tomb.) She looked me up and down as though I were a large bag of horseshit that some thoughtless groom had left on her carpet. I catch on quickly, and I already knew that life at Middleham was going to be one big barrel of laughs. She didn't like my curtsey. Christ, she had me curtseying for a whole week until I got it right. Then we started on the kneeling, because she said it was a skill necessary for those who took part in Court ceremonial. There's nothing more fun than kneeling for four or five hours at a stretch with your back straight. Yes, after that you really feel like dancing the night away.

You may think that I didn't much take to Anne, Countess of Warwick and you'd be dead right. As for her husband, Richard Neville, the Kingmaker, what can I say of him that hasn't already been said? He was tall, broad, and full of crap. To hear him talk you'd have thought that he, single-handed, had put King Edward on the throne, and that he, single-handed, was now running the country.

Things were still pretty lively in Yorkshire in those days. One of Margaret of Anjou's bright ideas had been to give Berwick away to the Scots in return for their help. This help came in the form of many violent raids across our borders, in which they were aided by sundry villainous thieves of the Lancastrian persuasion. Every so often, in addition to this, some little group of Mad Harry's followers would sneak into some poxy Northumbrian castle and hold on to it until Warwick and his brother, John, Lord Montagu, could get round to grabbing it back. They were great days for men who were tired of life.

You can see how I had come on in a short time. Instead of sitting in a Lancastrian castle worrying about falling into the hands of the Yorkists, I was sitting in a Yorkist castle worrying about falling into the hands of the Lancastrians. Yes, we were definitely building a better world.

After a couple of years the fighting began to ease off. We Yorkists had won.

There was already a new storm brewing. News came to us that the King had married, in secret, one Elizabeth Woodville.

Warwick was not a happy bunny when he heard of this. People often talk about someone dancing with rage, but this was the only time in my life that I saw a man actually do it, and that man was the Kingmaker. You see, as far as he was concerned, the King had no right to do anything at all without consulting the Earl of Warwick. Yet Edward had married himself to an obscure Lancastrian widow who was the best part of ten years his senior. A woman with no money, lots of greedy relatives, and no influence abroad. Boy, did Warwick dance. I don't know where he learned the steps, but if he'd entered the competition at Masham Fair he'd have won by a mile and a half.

Everything was smoothed over for a time, but it didn't take long for Warwick to find fresh grievances. He collected them as his main hobby, and always liked to have more than anyone else.

One day I was up on the battlements taking the air. (Middleham is a very good place to do that. There's plenty of air. Plenty of sheep. Not much else.) I was minding my own business when along came young Rob Percy, one of Warwick's numerous esquires.

"Any chance of a poke?" he asked.

"A poke in the eye, you horrible brat," I snapped back. "For one thing, you're a snotty little boy who couldn't squeeze enough out to father a mouse. For another, I have every intention of keeping myself pure for my future husband. For a third, I'm wearing a *clavette*."

He grinned. "No offence meant, Nell. I mean, you can't blame me for trying, can you? A man's expected to try. Is it uncomfortable? The *clavette*?"

"Oh, no," I answered, with a subtle hint of irony, "it's just like a second skin. Every girl's dream is to have about five pounds of steel padlocked around her middle. Didn't you know?"

"I'm sorry," he said, still grinning. He was one of those intensely irritating people you just cannot abash, no matter how much you try to embarrass them. He had bright red hair and a face full of freckles. "Listen, Nell, do you know that we've a newcomer in the household? Do you know who it is? Richard of Gloucester, the King's brother."

"Am I supposed to be impressed?" I asked.

"Yes. You haven't seen him yet. I have. He's a dwarf with a hump on his back."

"Come on," I said. "Everyone knows that King Edward is incredibly handsome. He's six feet four inches tall, with the biggest biceps in Europe. How can his brother be a dwarf and a hunchback?"

"I dunno," shrugged Robert, "but he is."

However, when I saw Richard of Gloucester for myself I discovered that while he was indeed only a slightly built lad, with the traditional acne, there was no sign of any hunchback. I later learned that it was very much a matter of posture, what Lady Warwick called deportment. In certain lights, when he slouched, Richard appeared to have a hump on his back. But he didn't really have one at all. That's my theory, anyway, and you may do with it what you will.

The trouble with Richard was not that he was hunchbacked but that he had no sense of humour. I shall spell that out to save you from any doubts. NO SENSE OF HUMOUR AT ALL.

That Christmas we had a troupe of players up from York to entertain us. They were about as entertaining as toothache until one of them seemed to make a mistake, and set his costume alight with a torch. You should have seen the leaping that brought on! The hall rocked. Everyone was pissing himself, from Warwick down to the scullions peeping in from the kitchens. Alianore Audley, damosel, fell backwards off her bench, shattered her hennin, and knocked Rob Percy, esquire, off his feet, so that the wine he was carrying spilled everywhere. Even Warwick's daughters, who always looked as if someone had just given them a very nasty shock, were giggling and gurgling like a pair of moorland streams. And Richard of Gloucester? What did he do? He picked up a cloak that Lord Scrope of Bolton had left lying around, strode into the middle of the hall, and rolled the player in it, smothering the flames. That's Richard summarised for you. It never even occurred to him that it might all be part of the act. I don't think Scrope was too pleased when he got his sable cloak back with a bloody big hole burned through it, but as the King's brother had done it I suppose he had to regard it as an honour.

The King's other brother, George of Clarence, was a different sort entirely. He'd laugh and joke with the best. Yes, he'd charm the birds out of the trees – so he could wring their necks.

Clarence came courting Warwick's elder girl, Isabel. She was well taken with him, and you could see why. He had a handsome face, and winning ways, and he was (at that time) King Edward's heir. The fact that he was rarely sober for more than an hour at a time didn't seem to trouble her.

Early one morning I found myself combing out Isabel's hair. She kept me at it for ages, because she had read somewhere that hair needed a hundred and fifty strokes of the comb at each session to keep it at its best. You get all the fun jobs when you're a young damosel in someone else's household. (Don't ask me why she was so worried about the condition of her hair when it was all going to be hidden under her hennin anyway. Isabel was that kind of person.)

"I'm *so* in love that if the King will not give his permission for me to marry Clarence then I shall just *die*," she said dreamily. By the way she was staring at herself you'd have thought that she was in love with the looking-glass.

"No, you won't. We don't die that easily."

"Then I'll go into a convent."

"You must be joking! They never waste an heiress on God. Your father will just find you someone else."

She frowned. She was good at that. I think she learned it from Warwick himself. "The trouble with you, Alianore, is that you've never been in love with anyone. You don't understand."

"I understand perfectly," I said, "and that's why I'm not such a damn fool. Sooner or later my brother Audley is going to find me a husband, and when he does I'm going to have to make the best of it. I shall fall in love with the man I'm given, instead of wasting the rest of my life mooning over someone I can't have."

"Alianore! He could be old, or fat, or ugly. He could have horrible breath. He might beat you. He might even be someone who doesn't know how to dance."

"As long as he isn't short of a few shillings, that's the main thing. And don't tell me that you'd love Clarence if he wasn't a duke and one of the richest men in the country, because I know you wouldn't."

She pouted angrily. "That isn't fair. Even if George was only an earl like Daddy, I'd still want him."

You only had to scratch Clarence's skin to find solid pork. I found myself beginning to feel sorry for Isabel. Not that I could do anything about it, you understand.

We had started to make preparations for the wedding when word came up from London that King Edward had forbidden it. Isabel didn't die in consequence, but she wept in her room for about three and a half weeks as she thought about that duchess's coronet slipping away. Meanwhile, her father was stalking about the castle muttering under his breath and biting big chunks of stone out of the walls.

Warwick and Clarence busied themselves drawing up a whole fresh list of grievances, and began to plot against the King. It was still a long-term plan, but their idea was to put Clarence on the throne. (With Isabel as Queen, of course. And her daddy pulling all the strings. Warwick didn't explain this last bit to Georgie. I expect it slipped his mind.)

If Warwick had troubled to ask me (which of course he didn't) I could have told him that he had more hope of turning the courtyard puddles into claret wine. You see, England was divided into three camps: those who thought that Edward IV was the rightful King; those who supported Mad Harry VI; and those (the great majority) who didn't give a toss either way. No one (except Clarence) wanted Clarence to be King – how on earth can you have a King called George?

One of the advantages of being a woman, and especially a young damosel, is that almost everyone thinks that you are stupid, and deaf to boot. I would be sat next to Lady Warwick in her solar, my head bent over my embroidery or whatever, and George and Warwick, only three or four feet away, would be openly plotting their treasons. Not even troubling to lower their voices. Amazing, I know, but true. I doubt whether they even noticed that I was there, and if they did they certainly didn't care. Some of the things they said about King Edward made my hair curl to such an extent that I could feel the hennin lifting off my head.

When I decided that matters had gone far enough, I wrote a long letter to my brother Audley that had, shall we say, the odd interesting fact in it. Rob Percy happened to be going into York on Warwick's business, and I gave him this letter to carry for me, knowing that he'd have no trouble in finding someone there to take it south. You may think that this was a pretty low trick, informing against Warwick and using his own esquire to carry the tale, but, as the saying goes, loyalty bound me.

It was about a month after this that a new face in the hall caught my eye. Warwick always had plenty of guests, of course, most of them eager to lick his backside in the hope of gaining one favour or another, but this man stood out from the crowd. Why he stood out I am not sure, unless it was that his clothes spoke of the Court.

"Who is that?" I asked Alice Savage, who happened to be sitting next to me.

"Who?" Alice was day dreaming as usual. I was always having to give her a sly kick to bring her back to reality. Lady Warwick didn't much care to be ignored, and her anger wasn't particularly selective, so it paid to keep the rest of the team in line.

I tilted my hennin in the appropriate direction. "Between Isabel and Lady Scrope."

"Oh, him!" cried Alice, the light of understanding dawning somewhere deep below the surface. She broke off a piece of lamprey and stowed it in her capacious mouth. "That's Roger Beauchamp. My lady's cousin. Cousin in some degree, anyway. Doesn't show up much in these parts. He's in the King's service, not Warwick's."

"I did rather gather that from his livery collar," I said, irritably. "You don't happen to know the length of his rent-roll, do you?"

She shook her head. "No. He's got nice eyes, though."

This was true, although it was scarcely to the point. Alice was the sort who never noticed the really important things about a man.

Much later that evening I was sent to the solar to fetch a book of recipes for the Countess. She had had a dispute with Lady Scrope about the best means of preserving parsnips, or something equally exciting, and decided that the only way to solve the issue was to look it up. The volume in question was a great, thick thing, bound in red leather, which had come down to her from her paternal grandmother, and was emblazoned with the Beauchamp and Ferrers arms. This should have been easy to find, and it would have been if it had been in its proper place instead of buried under seven cushions, a bundle of accounts, a lute and an abandoned embroidery project.

Middleham is a strange castle, quite unlike any other I have seen, although very luxurious. The solar is across the courtyard from the rest of the principal apartments, and linked to them by a wooden bridge. The bridge is roofed, of course, and glazed, but the timbers have a funny way of squeaking and bending under your feet, and you always wonder if you're going to make it to the far side. As I stepped off this bridge someone took hold of my arm. It was Roger Beauchamp.

"Unhand me, Sir!" I snapped. (I'd always wanted to say that. This was my chance.)

"What is a fair damosel like you doing in a dull household like this?" he asked.

He was older than I had thought at first sight, a good ten years my senior, and his hair was already thinning at the front.

"At the moment," I said, "I'm taking this book to my lady, and I've already been longer about the task than I should have been. She doesn't score very highly on patience, and I could cope with a few less fools blocking my way."

He gave me a winning smile. His teeth were in pretty good condition, I noticed, and there was not a single pockmark on his face. And he had good legs.

"I need to speak to you," he murmured.

"The custom of this household is to avoid idle dalliance except on Tuesday afternoons," I said lightly. "In any event, I don't suppose you wish to tell me anything that I haven't already heard. I've got a whole sheaf of poems under my pillow. I'm fully briefed on the colour of my eyes and the shape of my instep, and threats of imminent suicide do not impress me."

"Don't flatter yourself, Mistress Alianore Audley," he snorted. "I'm not here for dalliance, idle or otherwise. This is the King's business."

"Well," I admitted, "that is a new line. I've never been part of the King's business before. I *do* feel important. Have you written your poem yet?"

He jerked a thumb towards the nearest staircase. "The battlements, at midnight," he instructed. "Don't make the mistake of keeping me waiting, or you'll discover that I'm not one of your love-sick boys."

"It may not be that easy to get away," I objected.

"Be there!" he said, remorselessly.

It was one of those cloudless nights when it is not so much cold as bloody freezing, especially when you are stood on top of Middleham Castle with the north-west wind blowing in hard all the way from Fiend's Fell. I had my mantle wrapped tight about me, but, in all honesty, I couldn't have been much more chilled if I'd been stark naked.

Roger stepped out of the shadows, grinning his approval. "So, you decided to come," he drawled.

"I'm always turned on by men who threaten me," I said, fighting hard to stop my teeth from chattering.

"You're cold."

Observant fellow, I thought. "No. I'm a block of ice on legs. It has something to do with getting out of bed at midnight and wandering about on the roof."

"Come here," he ordered. He was used to telling people what to do, that much was certain. As I hesitated, he snatched at my wrist, pulled me close, and enfolded me in his big cloak. It was rather like being in a very small tent with him, with only our heads sticking out.

"The King wishes you to know that your loyalty is appreciated," he said. His voice was mellow, and rather grave, pleasant to my ear as well as very close to it. "Your report confirmed much that was already suspected, and you are to keep your brother Audley informed of developments."

"Is that all?" I asked.

"Is it not responsibility enough for a saucy young damosel? What did you expect? To be made Warden of the West March?

There's this as well." He pressed a very thin book into my hand. "It's an official enciphering manual. Put the serious stuff into code before you send it, in case it falls into the wrong hands. And, whatever you do, don't lose the manual, or let anyone else see it. We don't want any harm to come to you."

"I didn't know you cared," I said.

He grunted. "I am a knight. It is my sworn duty to protect all ladies and damosels, even those I don't particularly like."

"Good God," I cried, "have you ridden directly from Camelot, or did you take the long way round? You'll be telling me next that a knight's word is never broken, and that he loves his honour better than his life. And, of course, that he serves his lady without the least thought of swiving the butt off her."

"Alianore," he said, patiently, "you do very ill to mock the Knightly Code. I think the time has come for you to go back to bed."

I didn't want to go back. I'd grown comfortable where I was, warm and secure, and it was rare sport to provoke him.

"Are you a wealthy knight?" I asked. "Tell me about your property, and any inheritances you have pending. If it's a long enough tale I might just allow you to carry me off. I need a change of air and a new challenge."

"I know exactly what you need," he assured me. "Do as you are bid, and go to bed. Now."

He withdrew his cloak from around me, so that the chill rushed back into my very bones. I decided it was too cold to argue, and so I did as I was told.

Warwick's next error was to try to draw Richard of Gloucester into the plot, using his younger daughter, Anne, as bait. I was present for this interview as well, so I might as well tell you about it.

We were gathered in the solar at Middleham.

Warwick stood with his back to the fire, keeping all the benefit of it to himself. He was making an enormous effort to appear relaxed and avuncular. He kept trying out his smile on one of the dogs.

Isabel had assumed a pose. (My mother used to say that that was the only thing that any woman should assume, especially where men were involved.) She was, I think, trying to determine the correct angle of backward tilt for her head and the exact arrangement of folds for her skirts. She knew that if she could impress Richard of Gloucester she could impress anyone.

Anne stood next to her sister. She was twelve years old, but could have passed for younger. She'd been given a good scrubbing and a new gown, and been allowed, nay, told to wear her hair loose. It was long and blonde, and definitely her best feature.

Lady Warwick sat by the window, working on a big piece of embroidery she had in her frame. I was on hand to thread her needle, sort out her silks, plump her cushions, chase away the dogs, and do whatever else I was told to do. Alice Savage was at a lectern, reading aloud from a book of poetry, and Rob Percy, wearing the cleanest livery his back had ever known, was on hand to pour out the wine when required. It was all very cosy and domestic.

Richard walked into this tableau, and Warwick and the Countess gave him the sort of welcome he'd have merited if he'd just arrived from Jerusalem instead of the henchmen's dormitory. You could see Gloucester cringe, and the hump swelling on his back. Richard never liked much in the way of fuss, and there they were, laying it on thicker than an old whore's face paint.

Warwick was subtle at this point. I'll give him that. He said a lot about reforming the government and removing the advisers who had an unfortunate influence over the King. Not much at all about chaining Edward in a dungeon to starve to death and putting good old George in his place. Then he began to rattle on about the past, reminding us all that he, Warwick, had loved the House of York all the way back to his days as an embryo, and how his own father, Salisbury, and Richard's father, York, had both died in the common Yorkist cause, at the hands of the bloody bitch Margaret of Anjou.

King Edward, he said, had forgotten the old ties of blood and kinship. Edward cared only for his Queen and her swarm of grasping Woodville relatives, and preferred men who had fought against him above those who had fought for him. He had to be won back to the correct way of thinking. (Warwick's way, Warwick meant.)

My legs were growing tired. I shifted my weight, and prayed for it all to end. I noticed that Isabel was still holding her pose. (She could easily have been replaced by a wall painting; it would have saved some expense.)

"We can best persuade Edward as a united family," Warwick went on. "George is to marry Isabel. You're as good a man as your brother. Why not tie the knot with Anne at the same time?"

"The King's forbidden it, that's why not," Richard answered.

"Then he can flaming well *unforbid* it!" Warwick yelled, so loudly that Isabel jumped back six inches without losing her pose. Anne started to cry, although exactly why was not clear to me, she being far less interested in ducal coronets than was her sister.

"How you do run on, Cousin," said Gloucester, without raising his voice. He was very composed for a lad of his age. "You know right well that he will not."

"He *will*!" cried the Kingmaker. He actually stamped his foot. "Sooner or later he will. If it comes to a choice between Warwick and the Woodvilles, only a damned idiot is going to choose the Woodvilles. That includes Edward, boy, and it most assuredly includes you."

Richard drew himself up to his full, unimpressive height. (I could slouch and still stand taller than him, without counting my headdress. So could Anne, even then.)

"Ah, all that's coming out of you is a load of wind, Warwick," he said.

You can see why, in later years, the men of Yorkshire took to Gloucester so well. They like straight talk in that part of the world.

Richard didn't stay with us very long after that. Nor was I very far behind him. Warwick had friends at Court, and it soon came to his ears that Lord Audley had been stirring it down there. Warwick was the sort to take things like that personally. John went on the long list of people that he wanted to behead. It took him about a week and a half to figure out that I was Audley's sister. You could almost hear the cogs turning in his head. He gave word, through his Countess, that I was to pack my boxes.

This was a real blow to me. It'd been a joy living with Lady Warwick. After all, she'd never beaten me except when there was a *d* in the name of the day. Yes, if someone had only thought to present me with half a dozen raw onions I reckon I could have had a really good cry.

I had about a month at home in Shropshire before I was summoned to Court. This was a good career move. I didn't need asking twice.

III

"You're twenty-one," said John, meaningfully.

"Yes," I agreed. Thinking, so, you can add up.

"Pushing twenty-two."

"Yes."

"High time you were wed."

"Has someone asked for me?" I asked, hoping that they hadn't.

"Not yet. But for Christ's sake, wench, if you can't find a husband at the King's Court you're too lazy to make an effort. Get on with it!"

You'll notice that John had been cured of his cold by this time. But he was still on a bit of a short fuse. I didn't want another smack across the mouth, so I said that I would. Get on with it, that is.

The sort of offers I received weren't generally of marriage. As I'd just arrived from the country everyone seemed to think that I'd still got straw stuck behind my ears. You wouldn't believe the half of it but, I tell you, compared to some of King Edward's friends and relations, Rob Percy was a master of subtle seduction.

Even the King himself wasn't above having a crack. However, I must admit that once I had given him a friendly punch in the groin he recognised that the game wasn't on. He never held it against me again.

I dare say that if you went around the world you might perhaps find the odd king who took exception to being treated like that. Edward simply laughed it off. I think it made him like me the better. He really was as big and as charming as everyone made out.

As for the Queen, Elizabeth Woodville, it suffices to say that all the training Lady Warwick had given me in the fields of curtseying and kneeling came in real handy. Elizabeth was by far the most beautiful woman I ever saw in my life, but she had never heard about not standing on form. If there was a form, believe me, she wanted to stand on it.

I'd just about found my bearings at Court when the fighting kicked off afresh. Warwick and Clarence had organised a rebellion. Don't expect me to give you a blow-by-blow account. Look it all up in the Chronicles if you're that interested.

At one point King Edward was captured by the enemy, and things looked so bad that my brother Audley fell to studying the timetables of the ships to Burgundy. I think he even booked himself an open ticket, and with good reason, because Warwick had him marked down as a public enemy.

But then fortune turned our way again. Edward regained his freedom, and when all was done it was Warwick and Clarence and their womenfolk who had to dash for the ferry to France. (I should have mentioned that Clarence had married Isabel by this time.)

It was decided that there should be a grand tournament to celebrate, and I popped into the King's library to take a look at his copy of *The One Hundred Wealthiest English Knights*. I didn't want to bestow my favour on just anyone.

Richard of Gloucester was already there, thumbing through the latest edition of the *Court Circular*. He was studying the *Used Destriers* section, and wearing the troubled expression of a man whose bowels have not moved for three months. Richard always did look a bit like that. You got used to it after a while. Some women even found it attractive.

"It's good to see a face that doesn't belong to one of the damned Woodvilles," he said.

I shrugged. "I work for the Chief Woodville, but I hope it's only temporary."

I had aroused his sympathy. "Do you miss Middleham?" he asked.

"Like a chapped lip," I said, determined to be truthful. "The company, perhaps. Never the place."

"I miss the place, and the company." His sigh was so deep that it probably finished up somewhere in the vaulted cellar beneath our feet. "Warwick was always good to me. It wasn't easy, you know, to make that choice. My brother, the King, came first, but it was only by a short head. The shortest of short heads. The hairs on the horse's nose. Sometimes I wonder if I should have gone the other way, when I see the blasted Woodvilles, and all the other hangers-on, crawling out of every crack in the floor."

"Should you be telling me this?" I asked.

"No. But I have to tell someone. I gave up Anne, and the prospect of half the Warwick estates, and for what? I've not even been thanked."

"Well," I said, rather impatiently, "it's no use sitting around here and moping, Cousin. You aren't the only one who detests the Woodvilles and yet is loyal to the King. My brother Audley would be the first to offer his support, but there'd be plenty of others fighting to be next. You could be the leader of the third force in English politics."

"Politics!" he spat. "I'm sick to my teeth with politics! Do you know that Warwick is planning to marry Anne to Mad Harry's so-called son, Edward of Lancaster? He's spent the last twenty years calling Margaret of Anjou a bitch, a whore and a murderess, and now he agrees to give his own daughter to her bastard, such is his hatred for the King. That's where politics gets you."

"You mean that Warwick has turned Lancastrian?"

"Exactly that. And Lewis of France is their ally."

I sat down heavily. (I shouldn't have sat down, heavily or otherwise, without his express permission, but we were going easy on the etiquette that day.) I was gutted. The wars were not over after all. Uncertainty does nothing for any market, and the marriage-market is no exception to this rule. I knew that any husband I chose could be dead, attainted, and penniless within the year. My plans for my future were ripped up into small pieces and thrown off the battlements into a swirling wind. (I speak metaphorically of course. Eltham Palace doesn't have battlements worth mentioning, and it was a very still summer.)

When I had gathered myself together again, I strolled down to Garter King of Arm's office to get hold of the list of knights taking part in the tournament, and see what odds I could get on Richard of Gloucester.

Garter himself was out, doing whatever it is that Kings of Arms do on their day off, but his assistant, Bluemantle Pursuivant, was minding the shop.

"Your first big tournament, is it?" he asked, handing me a copy of the official programme.

"Yes," I said, "although I've been to a few county events, jousts at weddings, stuff like that."

He laughed at my ignorance. "Oh, those little affairs out in the sticks aren't worth talking about. A royal tournament is different class. You'll find it a very special experience. Do you want to be allocated a knight for the day?"

"I haven't really thought about it."

"It costs, but it's good publicity. You get to lead him into the lists at the end of a gold chain, and then he carries your favour on his lance. We can even arrange for a private room for you and the knight of your choice, with a bath and full supper, if you want to go the whole hog. The package comes complete with ointments, bandages and splints to bind up any little wounds he may have picked up. Very romantic."

It was at that moment that Roger Beauchamp put his head around the door. He was clutching a copy of the programme.

"Good morrow, Bluemantle," he said, cheerily. "What's all this about putting me on the Woodville team for the mêlée? I'm not a Woodville, and I'm not connected with the Woodvilles in any way, so it doesn't make a right lot of sense, does it?"

"Sorry, Sir Roger," the Pursuivant sighed. "They're pretty short of first-class knights, and we had to do something to shore them up, if you'll pardon the expression. If it's too one-sided we'll be buried in complaints from the sponsors, and the Queen'll be round here, banging on the counter like she was last time. It's more than my job's worth to let that happen again."

Roger's mouth opened to continue the argument, but then he caught sight of me and bowed his acknowledgement of my presence.

"Sorry," he said, "I didn't realise that there was a queue."

"I didn't even realise that you were at Court," I answered.

He did not take up my implied invitation to explain where he had been. He just mumbled something about being occupied by the King's business and left it at that. His evasiveness irritated me beyond all reason.

"The Damosel was about to pick her knight for the tournament," announced Bluemantle, rubbing his hands together at the prospect of income.

I stabbed my finger onto the programme more or less at random.

"Is he still available?" I asked, without looking down.

Bluemantle lifted my finger from the paper. "Sir Edward Woodville? Oh, yes. I can give you a discount on him."

Sir Edward Woodville was the Queen's horrid little brother, a vapid youth who spent most of his time slumped in corners, pulling the legs off flies. That's what random selection does for you. Before I could change my mind, Roger spoke up.

"I can't hang around all day, Bluemantle. Just get me off the Woodville team, that's all."

"The King won't like it, Sir Roger."

"Just do it, or I'll withdraw altogether."

He was as abrupt as that, and went stalking out of the room. It was as if I'd done something to offend him.

It was enormous fun sitting in the stands watching as my knight had the proverbial seven kinds knocked out of him. For some reason both Richard of Gloucester and Roger Beauchamp seemed determined to single him out, and Edward Woodville spent the rest of the week counting his compound fractures. He had to mend them himself, as I had only gone in for the basic sponsorship package.

That evening we had a great feast, and I sat and roared with laughter as a very amusing jester chap walked around the tables breaking wind and hitting us all on our heads with a pig's bladder. If there's one thing I really appreciate it's subtle, sophisticated humour.

Roger broke into the conversation I was holding with my sister Margaret, Lady Powys. (This Margaret was my full sister, and those of you who are fussed about such things should not confuse her with our half-sister, Dame Margaret Dutton, who was mentioned in my description of Blore Heath. Don't ask me why my father was so unimaginative as to give two of his daughters the same name. Or why he had another pair both called Anne. I haven't the foggiest idea.)

Roger informed me that I was a very poor judge of a knight, and that my favours should be bestowed with more care.

I told him that I would jolly well tie my sleeve to whatever lance I pleased, and that it was none of his bloody business.

He smiled, which was not at all the response I'd expected. This worried me.

He made a long and elaborate apology to Margaret for the interruption, using all the flowery language he'd learned at knight school. Then, without warning, his hand clamped on my wrist.

"Time for a little walk," he explained. "I need to have a quiet word with your brother. You are in need of guidance, Damosel. Perhaps we can arrange matters so that your behaviour will be my business."

John was sitting in a remote window embrasure, working on an account-book he'd smuggled into the banquet.

"Audley," said Roger, without preamble, "this is your advertisement in the *Court Circular*, isn't it?"

He pulled the *Circular* from somewhere, and held it about two inches from my brother's nose. John squinted at it.

"Yes," he admitted, after turning the page over a couple of times.

"And this is the damosel in question?"

"Only one I've still got on my hands."

"Then let's see if we can't cut a deal. Sit down, Alianore."

"Excuse me," I said, "but I'm getting a bit cheesed off with you telling me what to do."

"Stand up then. See if I care. Audley, what are you offering in the way of dowry?"

I sat down, somewhat shaken by the turn that events had taken. John had dropped the *Circular* on the bench next to him, and I found the relevant entry in the *Alliances Sought* section. It said: *Damosel, XXI years. Warranted chaste and obedient. No visible blemishes. Offers to John Audley, at Eltham. Woodvilles, Hautes, etc., need not apply.*

"Four hundred marks!" Roger roared, in response to John's first proposal. "You must be joking, pal. Obedient? She won't even sit down without an argument! And she's given her favour to a Woodville at a public tournament. I need compensating for the damage to her reputation. I want seven fifty, and not a groat less."

They hammered away at each other like two hucksters swapping stolen goods in back room of an alehouse, while I posed and pretended indifference. I was delighted that Roger had decided to put in a bid, but I sure as hell wasn't going to let him know that. I was going to have to be won round, and I was determined that it was going to take at least a week.

Roger was too astute to put all his cards on the table at once, but he threw them down one by one. He had an income of more than three hundred pounds a year from his lands alone, besides his retaining fees from the King, his salaries as a councillor to assorted lords and ladies, and the drops he received in return for bending things at Court for various people. He was in good physical nick, with a decent seeding in the jousts, and a childless widower, in need of an heir.

After about three hours, John contrived to beat Roger down somewhat on the dowry, and accepted the deal on my behalf.

"We'll have to get the lawyers in to agree the contract, of course," he announced, "but I don't see any problems. Welcome to the family, Beauchamp."

They shook hands, after John had spat on his.

"Do I have any say in the matter?" I asked, being the romantic sort.

"Alianore," Roger said, rather reprovingly, "of course you have some say. Do you think we're living in the Dark Ages? You get to choose your wedding gown."

A few days later John intercepted me on my way back to work from the palace chapel. "Beauchamp has withdrawn his offer for you," he said.

I awoke from my dreams with a nasty start. I'd thought it too good to be true.

"He withdrew it at my request," my brother went on. "He didn't want to stand in your way once I told him about the great good fortune that's dropped into your lap."

I didn't say anything. I didn't trust myself. The floor looked particularly dusty, and I didn't want to have to pick myself up from it.

"The new offer for you is truly exceptional," he said. "A once in a lifetime chance. Almost beyond belief. The King wishes to speak to you."

Oh, God, I thought, it's a ward or it's a reward. Either some little boy heir, still carrying the marks of his tutor's birch across his behind, or else some battered warrior with bad breath who's won the prize for killing the most Nevilles.

Richard of Gloucester was in the room with his brother. He began to look awkward as soon as I walked in. I swear you could see the hump growing on his back.

Edward seemed to be talking in Chinese. He wasn't of course. It was English, and the King's English at that. It was just that I couldn't make sense of it. He seemed to be saying that he wanted me to marry Gloucester.

I tapped myself on the side of the hennin, trying to make the wax drop out of my ears. No, it wasn't a joke, he really wanted me to be the Duchess of Gloucester. I had one prime qualification. I wasn't a Neville.

Boy, did I have to think quickly!

"No way!" I said.

I didn't look at John. I didn't need to. I'd heard the click as he'd unbuckled his belt.

"I'm not up to the job," I went on hurriedly. "For one thing, I'm not a virgin. I've been Lord Stanley's mistress for the last six months."

"You've been *what*?" This was John exploding. If there was one man on earth he hated it was Thomas Stanley. He'd not forgotten how our old friend had stood aside at Blore Heath. "Stanley's whore? You're no sister of mine!"

This was a really stupid remark. Of course I was his sister, albeit of the half-blood. We had the same father. But I suppose you understand what he was getting at.

Why did I tell this great big obvious lie? It was the first thing that came into my head, that's why, and there wasn't time for a better invention. I couldn't marry Richard. He was too young for me, and, besides, I knew that he had his heart set on little Anne Neville. What man in his senses would not fall in love with the heiress to half the Warwick estates? Anyway, I am not of the stuff from which duchesses are made. If you gave me more than half a dozen waiting-women I'd not know what the hell to do with them all.

The Monday following Cousin Edward sent for me again. I had the strangest suspicion that he wasn't planning to induct me into the Order of the Garter.

"Welcome, Cousin," he said. "I've a task for you. Your mission, if you choose to accept it, is to nip over to France and win George Clarence back to our side."

"What if I don't choose to accept it?"

He smiled. Edward had a lovely smile when he was putting pressure on you. "I happen to know a convent with a really nice line in punishment cells. With the full agreement of your brother Audley I've made you a provisional booking for six months. You've far too much colour in your cheeks, Alianore. Very unfashionable. A few weeks in a pitch-dark room would work wonders."

"I believe that France is quite pleasant at this time of the year," I said. "What do I have to do?"

"Hastings will give you your final briefing," he replied, grinning. He withdrew into the next room, where the Queen was awaiting him.

Will Hastings was the Lord Chamberlain, and Edward's bosom buddy. A real creep. He stepped forward, slid his arm around my waist, and led me over to a small table.

"This is your special equipment," he told me. There was a bag of French coins, a horn of invisible ink, and a garter with a knife in it. And a letter. "Careful with that," he said, lifting it up and waving it about. "It might explode. It's from Georgie's mummy, and she's just a tad cross with him."

"Is this all I get?"

"You'll have an escort as well. What more do you need? Intelligence reports indicate that Clarence should be willing to bite. Now that Warwick has done a deal with the Lancastrians, poor Georgie is left out in the cold. Redundant. Like the proverbial spare cock at a wedding. Persuade him to come home."

"How?"

Hastings grinned, and gently squeezed my right tit. "Think of something."

I told you he was a creep.

There were two men in my escort.

Guy was an archer *de la maison*. What's that? Well, he gets the same wage as an esquire, plus a house for his wife, and he can shoot the balls off a fly at a hundred paces. A useful chap to have around. Any more questions?

I didn't recognise Roger Beauchamp at first glance. He was disguised as a yeoman servant, with not a piece of shining armour in sight. We didn't want to attract too much attention, did we?

Roger was inclined to be a bit stand-offish. He'd heard the tale about Stanley and me, and was not overly impressed. He wasn't discourteous, or anything like that, but I sure knew he wasn't going to vote for me to be Damosel of the Year.

We were soon on the road to Southampton. To be honest, I was quite glad of the change. Life as a Court lady isn't all it's cracked up to be. I was sick of toadying to Elizabeth-I'm-too-sexy-for-my-hennin-Woodville. It involved too much wear on the knee joints. And once you've seen one tournament, brother, you've seen them all.

We landed at Barfleur. Roger carried me ashore, partly because I didn't want to get my feet wet, and partly because I had only just stopped sharing my breakfast with the seagulls.

"Put me down, my man, and go and hire some horses," I said, in my best, haughty voice. I hadn't waited on the Queen all those months without learning a few tricks. "Be quick about it, and don't let these Frogs cheat you, either."

It took ages to find where Clarence was staying. This was largely because none of the damned ignorant French peasants seemed to understand English. (They expect us to invade them every fifty years or so but they can't even be bothered to learn our language.) It turned out he was inland, at a place called Valognes. I decided that we had gone far enough, and halted outside a dirty little inn a few miles down the road.

"Help me down from my horse, varlet," I told Roger, still laying on the arrogance, "and then secure us some rooms in this unworthy dump. Fetch me a menu while you're at it."

He did. I read it while I was lolling on the luxurious comfort of my straw mattress. There was a marvellous choice. Either cabbage soup, or soup made from cabbages. They really know how to live, the French. No wonder that Henry the Fifth was so keen on the place that he went back year after year.

"I have the subtle impression that you've been trying to wind me up," said Roger.

"Does that trouble you?"

"Not at all. It's just that if you ever talk to me like that again, I'll pull you straight off your sodding horse and spank your arse."

"Promises, promises," I said.

"I'll remind you," he went on, "that I'm the one who gets to decide where we stay. I'm the leader of this expedition."

"What makes you think that?"

"Because I'm the only knight around here, that's what."

"You forget that I'm the King's cousin," I answered, leaping up and standing so close to him that our noses almost touched. "Moreover, I cannot possibly be seen to take orders from someone dressed as a smelly peasant."

"Tell you what. The next French herald we meet, we'll give him our pedigrees, and see who outranks whom."

"No need to be bloody sarcastic," I snapped. "After all, I never am."

There's nothing quite so romantic as a candlelit bowl of cabbage soup. Even now the mere whiff of the stuff makes me go weak at the knees. That's my excuse for what happened next. That and the fact that I'd left my *clavette* on the ferry. Well, I couldn't hold them all off forever, could I? I'm only flesh and blood.

"So, what you said about Stanley was a lie," Roger murmured.

"Of course it was a lie," I said, picking a hair out of his chest. "Mind you, I did dance with him once. That was bad enough."

I waited patiently for him to make sense of it.

"You invented the whole, wild tale so that you wouldn't have to marry Gloucester?"

I nodded. "Dead right. Quick, aren't you?"

He sighed, and shook his head. "I can see that I am going to have to watch you even more closely than I imagined, Mistress Alianore Audley. I knew that you were saucy. I didn't realise you were raving mad."

I smiled up at him. It was amazing how much more like a gentleman he looked without his clothes.

"Save your breath," I said. "As a helpless damosel I demand my right to be ravished repeatedly."

As my mother used to tell me, there's nothing better than a good knight in bed.

Clarence, as I said, was in Valognes, lodged in the castle. Warwick was away on business, finalising his dirty deal with King Lewis of France and Margaret of Anjou. My cover story was that I had come over to wait on Duchess Isabel.

I gave my business card to the porter. (I had a couple of dozen gross run off by that fellow Caxton, and they proved very useful. I'm sure they'll catch on.) Mine said:

Alianore Audley, damosel.

Queens attended. Kings cousined.

Tournament favours distributed.

Court intrigue consultant.

Embroidery commissions accepted – ask for quote.

"Hand this to your mistress," I instructed him.

"Aven't gor a mistress," he replied. "Aven't gor the bladdy money to go running arfter fancy women. Nor on my wages, I hain't."

"I mean to the Duchess of Clarence, you stupid pleb! Get on with it!" I was rapidly running out of patience, and that damned knife had dragged one of my stockings down to my ankle. So you'll understand that I wasn't in the mood for an amusing Cockney working-class character.

Isabel welcomed me, glad to see a familiar face. She was bored out of her head, and anxious for news about what everyone was wearing at Court, and who was currently climbing into bed with whom. When you're socialising with a duchess you generally have to let her set the tone of the conversation, and so I couldn't really get down to brass tacks.

Fortunately, it wasn't long before Clarence made an appearance, with the usual glass of wine in his hand, and I was able to give him the letter from his mother. He opened it, read about three lines, turned puce, and dragged me off into his closet for a private word. I don't know what the Duchess of York said in that letter, but I doubt whether she went over the top with compliments.

I told him what the crack was. That he was being given one last chance to return to his allegiance.

"What's in it for me?" he asked. His breath stank of malmsey. Come to think of it, you'd not expect it to stink of brown ale, would you?

"Your lands and titles. The love of your family. Fresh honours from Cousin Edward."

"What more?"

"A subscription to *Wine Drinker's Monthly*?" I suggested.

"Not enough," he grunted, pressing closer.

"Two weeks all-expenses-paid holiday at an Audley manor of your choice?"

Things were getting pretty heavy at this point. I did think of going for my knife. There were two problems. One was that he was holding both my hands in a vicelike grip. The other was that, on reflection, I didn't think that Cousin Edward would be too made up if I killed his brother, even a treacherous, worthless toad of a brother like Clarence. You can't be too careful when dealing with royalty.

I considered the possibility of introducing my knee to his gonads, a trick my mother taught me for use in dire emergencies. I was just about to give it a go when the door swung open, and in walked Warwick the Kingmaker himself. He'd just that minute arrived back from the French Court, his bargaining concluded, and it was obvious from his face that he thought he'd caught Clarence playing away.

"You're making enough noise to wake the dead," he snapped. "What the heck's going on here?"

"Nothing much, Father-in-law," said Clarence, rather sulkily. He shrank to his proper size under Warwick's harsh gaze, looking for all the world like a naughty schoolboy caught by the priest in the act of pissing up his grandfather's tomb.

"I know you," said Warwick, holding his finger under my nose. I noticed that the nail needed a good cleaning. "Never forget a face. Maud Roos, right?"

"Alianore Audley, my lord," I answered, curtseying.

"That's what I said. And what the hell are you doing here in France?"

"I'm here to serve Her Grace of Clarence."

"Oh, aye? And who was it as sent for you?"

"I did," said Clarence. This surprised me. Georgie was not noted for sticking his neck out for other people.

Warwick's jowls moved, as if he was chewing it over. You could hear the cogs turning again.

"All right," he answered graciously. "But see to it, wench, that it's the Duchess you do serve, and not this bugger. Do you hear me?"

I nodded, and Warwick sent me off to join Isabel. I breathed again.

Isabel was feeling very sorry for herself. She had thought that her father's intrigues were going to make her Queen of England, and she didn't like the idea of her younger sister getting the job in her place.

I played on her jealousy, and I played on George's hurt feelings. It took a few days, but, to be truthful, it was easy. Anyone could have done it. Clarence was always open to offers. He'd protected me from Warwick because he wanted to keep his options open. He soon agreed to write a letter to Edward, saying that he wished to come back into the fold, and I wrote one to

Hastings giving full details of Warwick's invasion plans. I gave them to Roger to carry back to England, because I had to stay with Isabel to avoid blowing my cover.

Next afternoon I was sitting on a window-seat with Isabel, helping her to untangle a skein of silk that she should never have tangled in the first place. I'll be honest, I was thinking of Roger, hoping he was safely at sea.

Warwick walked in. He had something in his hand.

"Messenger had a bit of a mishap," he said, throwing my letters on to my lap. They were covered with blood.

I stood up, and punched him, straight in the teeth.

"You stupid, brain-dead bastard," I cried, "you've killed your own wife's cousin."

IV

I've no wish to set myself up as an authority on dungeons of the world, but I reckon that those at Valognes would rate five stars in any guidebook for dankness, darkness, and deepness.

Yes, friends, Alianore Audley was up to her hennin in the solid stuff. I sat there wondering what they did to spies in France. I had an idea it would be something even worse than having to dance with Lord Stanley, or drawing Richard of Gloucester as partner for a joke-cracking competition.

They hadn't found my knife, and I tried to pick the lock with it. The blade broke in half. Typical English workmanship. Cheers, Hastings!

In the morning they led me into the adjoining chamber. Warwick was waiting for me, and with him an oily-looking young scrub. This, I learned, was Prince Edward of Lancaster, his new ally and prospective son-in-law. (The same Prince who, as a pretty little boy, had been touted around Cheshire and Shropshire by his dear mother, Margaret of Anjou.) In the corner, a chap with a hood over his head was stoking up a fire. I had a look at the implements on the wall, and realised that they weren't planning a barbecue. They weren't just going to pluck my eyebrows, either.

"Look," I said hurriedly, "there's no need to use any of this stuff. I'll tell you everything I know. I'll even tell you some things I don't know."

I think they were a bit disappointed, to be honest with you. I dare say that torturing a damosel would have brightened up their day. I gave them all the facts about my mission, and a bit more besides. I'm not the sort that gets a kick out of being hurt.

"Aye," said Warwick, thoughtfully. "It's just like Edward to send one of his tarts over to try to win Clarence back."

I don't know where Warwick got the idea that I was one of the King's tarts, as he so tastefully put it, but I can tell you it got me pretty wound up to hear him say it. After all, I was still practically a virgin. It's one thing to be threatened with sundry hideous torments, but to have your reputation questioned into the bargain is really a bit rich.

"And you still trust Clarence? After this?" asked the Prince.

"I trust none but myself. But I think I've shown young George which side his bread's buttered. No need to worry yourself, lad."

"What are you going to do with me now?" I asked, trying to sound bold. I wasn't sure that I really wanted to know the answer.

The Prince smiled. He was only about eighteen years old, but as nasty a piece of work as you'd wish not to meet.

"We're going to arrange for you to have a nice little swim," he said.

I was taken back to the dungeon. Quite a while later two French chaps came in. Big lads. Without so much as a by-your-leave they started to strip me, and before I could do them much damage they had me down to my shift. I thought that they were going to rape me, but it turned out that the mean-spirited bastards only wanted to steal my clothes. They left me the shift. The French are a funny lot, and I dare say that there's a law against throwing naked women into their rivers.

They made me walk upstairs with them to the guardroom, where they had a monk to hear my confession. I was about half way through my sins before they threw him out and sewed me into a big sack, with two large stones for company.

Was I afraid? You can bet your bottom groat I was!

The sack was picked up. I was thrown into a cart. We rattled through the streets. (I assume all this, because I was in no position to see.)

I felt myself lifted. There was a grunt, and I was pitched into space. There was a bloody big splash, and the icy water closed over me.

I kicked like buggery, as they say in Yorkshire. The sack, however, was strong, and didn't just fall apart at the seams as I anticipated. I'll be plain with you. At that moment I thought that I was riding sidesaddle to the big manor house in the sky. This, I thought, is how it feels to be an unwanted kitten.

Something grabbed me. It began to drag me towards the bank. It was Guy the archer.

I'd forgotten all about Guy. Luckily, he hadn't forgotten me.

"I took the two Frogs out just as they threw you," he told me. "Pity they dropped you on the wrong side of the parapet. Good job I can swim."

I coughed the water out of my lungs. It was dark, and we were sitting on a muddy bank outside the town walls. There didn't seem to be anyone else about.

"Honour forbids me to mix my blood with a mere peasant, or I'd reward you here and now," I said, still choking. "I hope you'll accept the cash alternative."

He grinned. "To be honest, Mistress Audley, I much prefer the earthy smell of a country wench. In fact, I'm a bit of a sheep-crap fetishist on the quiet."

"Well, if that's sorted, we'd better get on our way," I suggested. "The Frogs are likely to get a shade suspicious when they find those two punters with huge great arrows sticking out of them."

To all young damosels looking for a fresh experience I would say this: Walking around France in the dark wearing only a saturated shift is not something that I'd recommend. If you get the chance to do it, give it a miss.

Guy was more or less carrying me by the time dawn came up. He had the idea that we had to keep moving, and I knew he was right, even though I just wanted to lie down and die.

He left me under a tree while he went off to do a bit of scavenging. When he came back he had a bundle of clothes, a loaf of bread and a hunk of cheese. Apparently he'd stopped some people on the road, and a little friendly English diplomacy had persuaded them to co-operate.

The bread and cheese went down very well. I was less happy with the change of clothes, as they rather obviously belonged to a man. Still, they had one big advantage. They were dry.

"Nice legs," Guy remarked, when I stepped out from behind the tree.

"I feel like a complete prat," I said, angrily.

"You'll have to remember to keep your hood up," he added. "Unless you want to cut your hair short? Could you draw a boy's bow? If I can lay my hands on one?"

"My good man," I said, "I have shot at deer in the park at Middleham. Of course I can draw a bloody bow. Just as long as you don't expect me to hit anything."

"We've got to get back to England," Guy continued. "Warwick's planning an invasion. I reckon he'll be able to find room for a couple of extra archers."

We walked. Don't ask me how far. A hell of a sight further than I had ever walked before, that's for sure. (My idea of a long walk is from my horse to my place in the stands at a tournament.)

After only a few days of this we ended up at Barfleur. The place was swarming with soldiers, most of whom were in an angry mood because Warwick had forgotten to pay them. Funnily enough, this lack of cash did not stop them drinking. There was an Englishman lying in every gutter, and Guy had no trouble stealing a bow and a dozen arrows for me.

The ancient who recruited us asked us to take a shot each at a target he had set up. This was meat and drink to Guy. In one swift movement he notched his arrow in the bowstring and landed it in the dead centre of the gold.

My bow was only about a hundred and ten pounds pull. It was a hell of a struggle just to draw it, let alone take aim. The arrow flew out of my grip and split Guy's right down the middle.

I wish to make one thing very clear. That arrow could have landed anywhere from my left foot to the Isle of Wight. I claim no credit at all for skill. It was in fact the biggest fluke since Agincourt. I knew that. Guy knew that. Fortunately, the man signing us on for Warwick's livery didn't. He thought he'd just got hold of two chaps who'd been kicked out of Robin Hood's Merry Men for being better shots than the boss.

Warwick's army tramped the length of England, and we tramped with it. My feet were advising me to drop out of the game at this point, but I needed to get back to Cousin Edward and the one thing that was certain was that Warwick was taking us to him by the shortest route.

"We could get there quicker on horses," I pointed out, somewhere near Taunton. (We had already legged it from Plymouth, and I was growing shorter by the minute.)

"Sounds like a good way of getting our necks stretched," Guy muttered. Even so, he agreed to go along with the idea.

In the middle of the night we took a stroll down to the nearest horse park. There was plenty of choice, and only one man on guard. Guy sneaked up behind him, and held a knife to his throat.

"Keep quiet or you die," I told him. Then I looked into his face, and screamed my head off. Something I rarely do. It wasn't a man at all. It was a Goddamned ghost.

"Nice to see you again," said Roger.

I will be plain with you. I fainted. When I came round, the pair of them were laughing their heads off as they poured the second bucket of water over me.

Roger had been left for dead in a ditch, but Warwick's little friends had been too lazy to check on minor details. He had come round after a day or so, staggered to Barfleur, and copied my idea of signing on for the invasion.

Roger said that it was better for us to stay with the army for the time being. We could desert later, when we had less distance to run to join the Yorkists. So we tramped on, my blisters loving every mile of it. I didn't think I'd ever dance again.

My Cousin Edward was a Great King. His eventual record in battles read: Played six. Won six. The reason for this was that he was never too proud to run away when he knew that he was going to lose. Unfortunately for me, he didn't realise that he was going to lose until we had walked all the way to Coventry. We heard that he had fled to safety in Burgundy.

Those of us who were on short-term contracts were now given our pay and told to go home.

We three pooled our wages, and the other minor coins that had stuck to us on the road. We bought a cheap horse between us, and set off for Roger's manor in Gloucestershire, because the other two of us didn't have a home to go to. (You can imagine what John would have said to me if I'd rolled up at his front drawbridge dressed as one of Warwick's archers. The only question of doubt would have been which wall I'd have hit first.)

I got to ride.

I liked Horton Beauchamp immediately. It had a big bed, with a feather mattress and soft, clean sheets. I climbed in that bed and slept for about three and a half days. It took another three and a half days to comb the lugs out of my hair. And a week or so in a bath to soak all the aches out of my bones.

Roger's wife had died about five years earlier, bearing their son, who had also died. Her clothes were still folded in a big press in a corner of the room, and Roger told me to make free with them. They were a tad musty, a shade or two small for me, and about three reigns out of fashion, but it was better than being dressed as an archer, which was the only alternative.

I was in the middle of instructing a small party of Roger's men to scrape the twenty-seven inches of old rushes, bones, dog hairs, dead rats and assorted filth from the hall floor when he told me that he had just sent off a letter to my brother Audley to ask him to agree to our marriage.

"I hope that you've not ordered a couple of castles on the strength of the dowry," I said, stepping around the evidence that no one had troubled to let his dogs out that morning. "You'll probably have a job to find him. It's even money that he's currently lodged in an outside bog in Bruges. If not, he'll be hiding behind the arras at the Red Castle. I don't blame him, either. He's on Warwick's hit list like the rest of us."

"From what I hear, Warwick's trying to win friends and influence people."

"Yes, it was very conciliatory of him to have me sewn in a sack and thrown in the river. That's what I call meeting people half way."

Warwick had a bit of a task on his hands, ruling England on behalf of Mad Harry, with only such dubious colleagues as George Clarence and Thomas Stanley to assist him. Margaret of Anjou and Edward of Lancaster were still lingering among the Frogs, and there were plenty of Lancastrians who did not altogether trust friend Warwick, and were inclined to remain in the woodwork until such time as their precious Prince put in an appearance. Mad Harry himself, of course, was quite useless, just sitting there in his shabby royal robes, grunting from time to time and churning out the occasional prophecy. Poor man. He'd have made a first-rate hermit, but as a king he was a complete washout. England will have a major task to find someone less competent to rule her.

To my surprise a reply made its way back to us from John. He was lying low in Shropshire, but didn't seem to think that he was in any real danger. He gave consent to the marriage, and even went so far as to send Roger a dowry. Not much of a dowry, you understand, but enough to buy me a couple of new outfits and still leave sufficient to pay for the hall floor to be tiled.

I'll not trouble you with a description of the wedding, except to say that in the absence of any one of my five brothers it was Guy who had the pleasure of giving me away.

I was Dame Beauchamp, not bad promotion for a common archer. Roger and I started working our way through Brother Baldwin's *One Hundred and Twenty-six Positions for Knights and their Ladies*. (I like number V best, although number XVIII makes a pleasant change in the summer months.) Life was sweet again.

One morning, just as we were in the middle of number XXXV, there was a discreet cough outside the bed curtains. It was Guy.

"Great news, Sir Roger," he shouted. "King Edward has landed in Yorkshire!"

It wasn't great news from where I was lying. Roger didn't even bother to finish the task in hand. (Not that it was in hand, if you catch my drift.) He extracted himself from me, and vanished through the curtains.

"Where's my armour?" he demanded. "Has that idle bastard Fitzwilliam repaired the dent in my bascinet? Alianore, have you seen my battle-axe?"

"In my sewing-box, between the green thread and the thimble," I answered, a touch irritably. "Where do you think it is?"

Give a man a chance to go off to war and get himself killed and all else flies out of his head. It was as if he could no longer see me. As if I had suddenly become a ghost. However, just before he left, he took me to one side.

"Do you remember that you promised to obey me?" he asked.

I shook my head. "No. I think the priest must have forgotten that bit."

"You're to stay here. You are out of the way, and safe. Whatever happens, whatever rumours you hear, stay here."

"You've no need to worry," I said, "I know when I'm well off. I'll not wander the roads again. You've more chance of finding George Clarence sober."

The next thing I heard was that Warwick had come to a sticky end at the Battle of Barnet. We Yorkists were on top of the pile again.

George Clarence, I should mention, had managed to fight on the same side as his brothers. I still wonder whether it was that letter from his mother that did the trick, or whether it was just that he didn't like to wear the same coat for more than a few months at a time. Anyway, he turned Yorkist again, and left the Kingmaker well and truly in the lurch.

No sooner was Warwick dead, however, than Margaret of Anjou and her charming son landed at Weymouth with another Lancastrian army, and they started to march in the direction of Gloucestershire.

Something told me that I should begin to march away from Gloucestershire.

I stayed. I wanted to obey Roger, and I was very content where I was. After my little trip to France I was in the mood to appreciate a summer spent in the garden of a Cotswold manor house, believe me. Besides, Horton Beauchamp is not exactly on the road from anywhere to anywhere. You have to know where to look for it. Or get lost.

Prince Edward of Lancaster, who was too tight-fisted to hire someone competent to show him his proper road, got lost. He arrived just at the time when I was all out of boiling oil. Keeping him company was a whole army of cider-swilling wretches from Devon and Somerset.

He looked at me strangely, as if he could not quite place me.

"My wife is ill," he announced, in his cold, maniac's voice. "You will attend her."

They carried Anne up from her carriage, and laid her in my bed. She was ill, right enough. By the look of her that young pig had been using her as a punch bag. From what I could gather, she had made the mistake of weeping for her father.

Once I had calmed Anne, and settled her to sleep, I ventured down the stairs. The bastards were ransacking my stores, helping themselves to anything that could be lifted. The Prince was standing by the fire, with his mother, the Duke of Somerset, and old Lord Wenlock. Wenlock was in the act of splintering one of my chairs and adding it to the blaze. Now, there was a mild chill in the air, but it wasn't anywhere near cold enough to justify burning the furniture. He was just doing it to show what a big man he was.

The eldest of my full brothers, Sir Humphrey Audley, had arrived while I was upstairs. After we had recovered from our mutual surprise he promised me he would see to it that our brother Lord Audley and my husband were hanged from the same beam. After which he would make appropriate provision for me. He spoke rather as if I was one who had been deluded into the company of thieves.

Queen Margaret was another amiable sort. (Her father, by the way, called himself King of Jerusalem, Naples, Sicily and Aragon, although not one of the kingdoms recognised him as such. If there's one thing I can't stand it's a man who claims to be King of this and that when he isn't really King of anything. It's so frightfully middle-class.) The flatterers surrounding her, most of them old enough to know better, kept on talking about her achievements. What achievements? I wondered. Buggering up the country? Does that count as an achievement? When she was in charge she made more mistakes than a hedgehog in a brush shop. It's a miracle that she didn't go completely mad and introduce a poll tax, like King Richard the Second did in the old days.

I don't find it easy to make polite conversation while my house is turned into a pigsty around me. I dare say this shows a fault in my breeding, but that's the way it is. I also noticed that the Prince was still trying to work out where he had seen me before. I wondered when it was going to click with him, and decided it was time to make an exit.

I went back to Anne. She was awake, and shivering.

"I thought it was him," she said. She stared at me. "You are Alianore Audley, who used to be with us at Middleham."

"True," I murmured, "but do me a favour and keep it to yourself. The last time I bumped into your husband he tried to have me drowned."

"Drowned? For why?"

"For being a Yorkist spy, over in France."

"A Yorkist spy? You?"

"Yes. But don't worry, I've retired now. I've decided it's safer to specialise in embroidery and childbearing like everyone else."

"King Edward," said Anne, thoughtfully, "is only in Malmesbury. With Richard. Only a few miles away, isn't it?"

"About ten."

"Perhaps even closer, if he's learned that our advance guard is camped on Sodbury Hill. He should have done by now. That was the idea, to draw him there."

"To give battle?"

"No. The plan is to leave here, and Sodbury, in the middle of the night. To steal a march on Edward, at least five or six hours. "'Twill give us time to get across Severn, either at Gloucester or at Tewkesbury."

"Not at Gloucester," I said. "My husband's kinsman, Richard Beauchamp, is holding Gloucester for King Edward."

"At Tewkesbury, then. Once in Wales, we'll be joined by Jasper Tudor's men. A great multitude they say."

I knew that my Cousin Edward would pay richly for this information. It was just the minor detail of getting it to him.

"I might go for a ride later," I said, "if you've no objections."

There was a thick ivy growing up the wall below the solar window. It was just about strong enough to bear my weight. Court ladies do not generally have to descend from high windows without the aid of a ladder and at least a couple of esquires. If we did, we'd wear more practical clothes. It was a hell of a struggle to get down, and I tore my gown in the process. Good job it wasn't one of the new ones.

The courtyard was quiet. I had deliberately waited until the snoring had started, and a little while longer after that. I began to move towards the stable. As I did, the door opened, and men started to lead horses outside. I suddenly remembered what Anne had said about them leaving in the middle of the night. I'd obviously dozed off and left things too late. The menials were astir.

I took the deepest breath of my life. I picked up my skirts and sprinted for the nearest horse, which happened to be the Prince's. It was seventeen hands if it was an inch, and you could have shoved a pint pot up either one of its nostrils. Anyway, I vaulted straight into the saddle. What's that? You don't believe that I could do that? Listen, *I* don't believe it, and I was there to see it. It's amazing what the body will achieve when it realises that it's liable to have some very nasty things done to it if it doesn't make the grade.

I grabbed the reins from the lad who was holding them. He was another one who didn't believe it. There was a section of curtain wall that had fallen down during the last frost. I was over it faster than you can say *Blanc Sanglier*. A great deal faster, in fact, than if you try to say it while drunk. Robin Hood, eat your heart out.

It was hard work managing that destrier. It would have helped to have had twice my weight and three times my strength. I had to make do with promising him an apple if he was a good horse.

I realised that I was going to have to pick my way around the enemy forces on Sodbury Hill, but at least I had the advantage of knowing the ground. It also helped that they were already in the process of moving off in the general direction of Gloucester, and not much interested in looking for Alianore.

I'd just decided that I had got away with it when I was challenged by a picket.

"Who goes there?" he demanded from the darkness. An imaginative question I always think. One that demands an imaginative answer.

"Lady Beauchamp," I shouted, narrowly resisting the temptation to announce myself as the Pope and the entire College of Cardinals.

"Come forward slowly. No tricks."

"You silly man," I said. (Or words to that effect.) "What tricks do you expect? Do you suppose I've got a couple of dozen archers hidden under my skirts?"

He kept his bill pointed at me, just in case. I noticed with relief that he had the White Boar of Gloucester on his sleeve. At least I'd found the right army.

"I am the wife of Sir Roger Beauchamp," I snapped, pushing the tip of his weapon away from my face. "Take me to the Duke at once! I've vital intelligence for him. And I'd stand well back if I were you. I'm only just about holding this God-damned horse."

"You'll have to wait. I've sent my boy for an officer."

After what seemed like an hour, mostly spent fighting the destrier, someone came pushing through the trees.

"God's Truth!" cried Rob Percy. "It's Nell Audley! What in the name of all the sheep of Jervaulx Abbey are you doing here in the middle of the night?"

"Waiting for the next carrier's cart to Bristol." I rapped back. It was blasted cold, sitting there on the Prince's destrier with the night wind blowing around my ears and through the huge rend in my gown. I was a little surprised to see Rob. I had still thought of him as Warwick's man, not realising that he had defected to Gloucester's service at some point. They had been good friends at Middleham, of course.

"She wants to see the Duke, sir," reported the guard.

"Come on, then," said Rob. "Let's wake him. This should be interesting."

I won't repeat what Roger had to say to me when he found me in Gloucester's tent, delivering my news. There are some words that are not out of place in a military camp, but which no lady or gentlewoman should allow her quill to form.

Richard thanked me for my trouble. There was a moment when I thought he was going to smile, but he didn't quite make it.

There was no sign of his hump. He even looked taller than usual as he escorted me to the King's pavilion.

Cousin Edward heard me out, and then gave a series of brisk orders to wake the camp and move off. His way of thanking me was to lift me off my feet and give me a big kiss, followed by a playful slap across my behind.

"We've got the bastards!" he bellowed, laughing. "There's only a ferry at Tewkesbury, and they'll never get their army across before we catch them. Well done, Alianore! I was going to fine Roger for marrying you without my consent, but I'll remit that now. You've earned it."

It took me a minute or two to realise that he was joking about the fine. At least, I think he was.

V

Once home I got out my sewing box and waited for Roger like a good wife. Three trips to chapel each day. Food for the poor at the gate. All that stuff.

I lost two brothers at the Battle of Tewkesbury. (Sir Humphrey Audley and my bastard brother, James, both of whom were slightly more Lancastrian than Margaret of Anjou.)

My brother John, Lord Audley, lost several pints of blood through fighting for York.

Wenlock was killed by Somerset, who believed (wrongly) that he had turned his coat half way through the fight. It served him right for burning my furniture.

Prince Edward of Lancaster died flying the field, slain by Clarence's men. (Some say that Richard killed him in cold blood, but that is a damnable lie. I had the truth from Richard himself, so I know.)

Most of the other Lancastrian leaders were dragged from sanctuary in the Abbey and beheaded. (Sir Humphrey Audley was one of them, I'm afraid.)

Margaret of Anjou and Anne Neville were captured and sent to London.

Poor old Mad Harry died in the Tower. "Of pure displeasure and melancholy." (If you believe that explanation, you'll believe anything.)

It was all over. Cousin Edward was safe again on England's royal throne. Free to get on with important things, like drinking, feasting, and playing hazard with Hastings for first crack at Mistress Shore.

Roger came home to me in a litter, sore wounded. The fool had only gone looking for the very thickest part of the fighting instead of volunteering to guard the baggage like a sensible human being. Several months went by before he was able to set foot to floor again.

In the interim George Clarence got up to his tricks once more. He wanted the whole of the Warwick inheritance for himself, and this meant that he had to prevent his brother Richard marrying Anne Neville. The girl had been put in his care, and he hid her away in a London cook-shop.

The fiendishly clever Georgie had forgotten one tiny detail. Anne was a lady. Indeed, as Warwick's daughter she had been brought up more or less as a Princess of the Blood. She'd never in her life had to comb her own hair or fasten up her own gown. I need hardly add that she had neither a Cockney accent, a red face nor rough hands, while no one had ever got around to training her to dish out mutton pies. In short, she did stand out just a scintilla. It took Richard all of three days to find her.

To my surprise, Roger and I were invited to the wedding.

It was a very quiet affair. In fact, they couldn't have kept it quieter if Anne had been six months pregnant. (She wasn't of course. Richard was not at all the sort to enter the lists until all the requisite trumpets had been blown. I don't know how he ever managed to father those two bastards of his. He probably received a royal command to do it, in writing, with the Great Seal of England attached.)

As I danced with Roger that night, he produced a smile that had me worried.

"Gloucester has offered me an appointment in his household," he told me.

"You are the King's knight," I objected. (I don't usually state the obvious, but this was a special occasion.)

"The King approves. He wants someone at Middleham whom he can trust."

"At Middleham? Bloody Middleham?"

"That's why we've both been chosen," he confirmed.

"Me too? Up there, in the twenty-foot snowdrifts? With the wind blowing off the fells and turning my face to leather? With no one to visit but the Fitz Hughs and the sodding Scropes of Bolton? You have got to be plucking my garter!"

He shook his head. His was still grinning. "Nope!"

"Look," I said, desperately, "if you're still angry with me for what I did before Tewkesbury I'm sure I can find you a whip somewhere. There's no need to be bloody cruel!"

"Middleham it is," he said, remorselessly.

I woke up next morning with a hangover that would have crept into George Clarence's top ten. When my maid combed out my hair it felt as if someone was playing a drum solo in the middle of my brain.

I'd just about reached the point where I could string three words into a sentence without a groan when I received a message that the King wanted to see me. Court etiquette prevented me from returning the first answer that came to mind.

The Chamberlain showed me into the Presence. He was very polite, but I caught him weighing me up, as if he wondered how much I'd fetch per pound. That was Hastings all over. He probably ran a brothel in his previous life.

Edward was sitting on his bed, chewing an orange. He stood up to greet me, throwing the fruit away. It sailed out through the open window and hit a passing Woodville.

"Ah, Cousin," he said, with a warmth that made me suspicious from the first, "so glad you could find time to drop in. I've never thanked you properly for the service you did me before Tewkesbury."

"Think nothing of it," I shrugged. "Any time."

73

"We remember that even when you were in Warwick's household you did your utmost to warn us of his treachery. We hope that you'll agree to continue to keep an eye open for our interests up at Middleham."

"You want me to spy on your brother?"

"Why not come straight to the point?" Edward laughed.

"The King is concerned that the Duke of Gloucester may come under unfortunate influences in the North," Hastings said. "The Duke's personal loyalty is, of course, unquestioned."

"I'll tell him that. I'm sure it'll make his week. So, in short, you *do* want me to spy on him?"

"Certainly not. The King wishes you to be responsible for the gathering of intelligence throughout the North. Scotland will also come under your wing."

"Lord Hastings," I said, "you are obviously winding me up to some tune."

"Not at all, my lady. The job is yours if you want it."

I could not have been more amazed if he'd proposed to offer me to the Sultan of Turkey in a straight swap for Jerusalem. My mouth had dropped open so far that if you'd been quick you could have stabled a horse in it. I calmed myself down by framing the obvious question.

"What about the pay and conditions?" I asked.

"You can rely on me to be generous," Edward grinned, chucking me under the chin. (I was probably expected to go all wobbly at the knees at this point. In all fairness he was very attractive, and if we'd both been free and he'd wanted to make me Queen of England I dare say I'd not have needed longer than a weekend to think it over.)

"All right," I said, "as long as my husband doesn't object."

"Roger?" Cousin Edward laughed. "It was Roger who suggested it. Said it'd keep you out of mischief!"

Why on earth Roger thought that I needed to be kept out of mischief I can't imagine. It's not as if I was ever the sort to cause trouble. However, the reality of life is that a woman has no choice but to obey her husband. Most of the time, anyway.

Middleham was no better than I remembered. The air of romance had not yet had time to settle over it. The only consolation was that we had some good friends with us in the household. Rob Percy was now one of Richard's chief officers, and so was Francis, Lord Lovel, another of Warwick's former esquires, and another joker. It was these two who set up the trick fountains in the pleasance, working from a book of plans Richard had brought back with him from Burgundy. After that, you always had to be careful where you stood to sniff the flowers, or you could get a very nasty shock. I find distinctly limited amusement in having several gallons of icy Yorkshire water unexpectedly shot up the inside of my skirts, but I suppose it wouldn't do for us all to laugh at the same things.

Richard and Anne were still uncertain of one another. He was very fond of her, it's true, but he'd married her to secure her inheritance and she'd married him because to be Duchess of Gloucester was a slightly better paying career than third assistant scullery maid in a pie shop. Despite what some people will tell you, it was neither a love-match nor a forced marriage, but somewhere in between, like most decent arrangements between sensible adults.

Roger and I were allocated a tower to ourselves, which caused some resentment, I can tell you. The top floor was given over to my work, and here I would sit, reading the information that came in from my agents in the field, or writing my regular report to Will Hastings. I had to avoid spending too much time up there. My official appointment was as one of Anne's women, and in a job like that it does look a tad suspicious if you never show your face in your lady's solar. Besides, in my experience people always develop serious doubts about anyone who seems to have a taste for the solitary life. Refuse to socialise with your colleagues in a noble household and it's not long before everyone from the kitchen turnspit to the lord of the castle is convinced that you're several blackbirds short of a full pie.

We did not, of course, spend all our time at Middleham, but most of the riding forth that had to be done to establish Gloucester as the biggest cheese north of Trent was done by the men, or a select group of them. We ladies usually had to be content with the odd trip as far as York, or the ultimate excitement of an excursion to the fleshpots of Sheriff Hutton. Roger and I were lucky if we got away to Horton Beauchamp for three months in a year. Richard could always find work for us, and was the type who thought nothing of asking us to drop everything and ride up from Gloucestershire, as if he imagined that we lived in the next castle down the road from him. The pretext was often some triviality, like the Scots crossing the border and burning half of Northumberland.

I eventually bore my husband three sons, Thomas, Richard and Henry, and one daughter, Constance, although not necessarily in that order. Children are all very well in their place, but they do tend to get in the way of one's professional commitments, and after the fourth I started to take regular doses of Tegolin's *Love Potion Number Nine*. Yes, I know that some ladies swear by lumps of wool soaked in vinegar, but personally I could never stand the taste, and besides, it's damned inconvenient to have to catch a sheep every time you fancy a little bit of horizontal jousting.

The one advantage of living in a great household is that there are always lots of women around who are only too willing to pick up spare children from the floor, wave rattles at them, wipe whatever needs wiping, and so on. At Middleham even the

Duchess was into this sort of thing, but I have to say that I was not. My own contribution to the co-operative nursery tended to be at the other end of the age group, as I was always on the look out for bright esquires and damosels to recruit for my intelligence work. You may find this hard to believe, but suitable candidates came along about as regularly as pink horses. Still, at least I can say that I taught many a northern clodhopper how to dance without standing on the skirts of his partner's gown, and many a taciturn northern wench to sparkle in company and sew a straight seam. No one can say that Alianore Audley has not done her bit for the Renaissance.

The Earl of Northumberland gave Richard a degree of hassle in the early days. This chap, whose full name was Henry Algernon Percy – a distant relative of that subtle charmer, Rob – had rather a high opinion of himself. Indeed, if it had been much higher they'd have needed to extend God's dais to make room for another throne. He didn't care for young Gloucester poking his nose into Percy affairs, pinching his retainers and so on, and he went into a frightful sulk. Letters flew here and there, royal commissions were set up, and after lengthy negotiations the bacon was carved up between the two of them. From then on Northumberland added to the many attractions of Middleham by becoming a regular guest. In my mind's eye I can still see him sprawling in the big chair next to Richard, swinging his Warden of the Marches badge about on its chain, and refusing to socialise with anyone below the rank of baron. I decided that he required some very serious watching, and included some malicious reports about him in my despatches to Hastings. I didn't actually hear him say that the Queen was an ugly old Lancastrian cow, but I'm sure he thought it, and so it wasn't really a lie to pass this on.

On the other side of the Pennines was my dear old friend Lord Stanley. He who had let the side down at Blore Heath. Now, in fairness to Thomas Stanley, he had not singled my father out for special treatment. He hadn't turned up at Barnet or Tewkesbury either, despite having served in Warwick's government. In point of fact he'd never shown his face at any battle worth mentioning, with the sole exception of Towton in 1461, where he slipped up and fought on the Yorkist side. I suspect that even there he was jolly close to the back, guarding the line of retreat or something.

Unfortunately, this particular flower of chivalry had enormous power in Lancashire, and had no wish to share it with Cousin Richard. He had a running feud with the Harrington family over Hornby Castle, and, to cut a long story short, Richard took sides with the Harringtons, who often dropped in at Middleham for a stag hunt and a couple of quarts of old ale. This led to some trifling scuffle. I was sitting on a window-seat at Middleham when it all happened, and so I'm afraid that I can't give you full details of the deployments, or of the tactics used. However, I understand that the technical term used by knights for what took place is 'A Complete Cock-up'. Anyway, Richard's own banner was lost, and carried off by the Stanley forces.

Gloucester was less than made up.

To make matters worse, a letter came up from King Edward, which made it clear that he backed Stanley in all this. He appointed Richard to head a Commission that was to force the Harringtons to give up the disputed lands! My briefing from Hastings said that some people thought that Richard was growing a shade too large for his boots. You could almost smell the Woodvilles on the paper. I discussed the intelligence despatch briefly with Anne before tearing it into quarters and hanging it on a nail in the garderobe. Why did I bring Anne into it? Because she was a hell of a sight brighter than she let on, that's why. I bounced everything of a delicate nature off Roger, or Anne, or both of them. They were both pretty shrewd judges, and depending on what they said I knew whether to (a) give Richard a direct security briefing myself, (b) give Anne the ammunition to fire for me, or

(c) just keep my mouth shut. (Option (c) applied in this case, if you're in any doubt.)

Intelligence reached me from a source in Lancashire, Sir Thomas Pilkington, that the captured banner had been hung up in Wigan Church. This had to be the ultimate insult. This meant war.

Roger reminded me that that was just what we had to prevent. We were there, after all, to protect the King's interests, and the King wanted peace in the North. The King, moreover, had made it quite clear that he favoured Stanley, and that he did not want Richard's power to increase at Stanley's expense. (This may strike you as a lousy bit of policy, but that's how it was. Moreover, Edward was neither the first nor the last king to go out of his way to keep Stanley sweet.)

Richard was livid. He wanted that banner back, and he wanted it straightaway. He proposed to gather together the biggest army he could muster, invade Lancashire, and take the place apart. (Or at least, those bits of the county that were owned by Stanley and his chums, a very fair proportion of the whole.)

"This could lead to some extremely negative vibrations from London, Your Grace," I told him.

(In my experience it's always wise to flash around a few honorifics when royalty has had a bad day.)

Richard had a nervous habit of twisting his rings on his fingers. At this point they were going around so quickly that I thought he was going to screw his hand off.

"I want that banner," he said fiercely. "If you've any better ideas on how to do the job, Dame Beauchamp, I'm prepared to listen to them."

Alianore, I thought, you've opened your big trap again. What on earth was I supposed to suggest? He stared at me, the lump on his back growing by the second. Anne kicked her embroidery frame over to create a diversion, but he didn't even glance at her.

"Roger and I will go over to Wigan and get it," I said.

Well, could you have come up with a better idea in the ten seconds allowed? If so, feel free to write your own version of the next chapter.

VI

Lancashire is a desolate county, largely made up of moors and mosses. A moss, by the way, is the local name for a peat bog. Wander off into one of those and it's a four to six shot that you'll never come out again.

I do, of course, exaggerate a shade. There are some rich pastures and wooded hills, and the people, if you can find any, are marginally more friendly than their fellows in Yorkshire, although their speech is every whit as difficult to understand. People in the North use their words as if each one costs sixpence, and much of their meaning is carried by grunts, nods and significant glances, or by the tone of voice. It takes time for a stranger to get used to this.

We stopped at Pilkington Hall to plan our strategy. Sir Thomas Pilkington was one of Richard's strongest supporters west of the Pennines, and no friend of the Stanleys. He'd served as Sheriff of Lancashire umpteen times, and I knew from the intelligence reports he sent me from time to time that he was no man's fool, even if he did wear something of a glazed expression.

Sir Thomas settled us down in his hall, where we could enjoy the smoke from the fire burning in the middle of the room. They hadn't quite got around to building chimneys in that part of the world. His daughter-in-law fetched us a tray of wine, and I realised that she was an old friend of mine, Alice Savage from Middleham. There was no immediate chance to talk because she was busy with her latest daydream and spilled half the wine down Roger. He was very charming about it, especially when Alice started to rub him down with her skirts.

"Stanley," Sir Thomas said, coughing, "has got so many men around Wigan Church that even the priest has a struggle to get in. There's no way that you'll sneak that banner out of there. It'd be easier to steal the fluff out of Stanley's purse. Why not start with something relatively straightforward, like popping over to France and persuading King Lewis to exchange his throne for a pack of lard and a Cumberland sausage? Haw! Haw! Haw!"

When Sir Thomas had stopped laughing, or coughing, or whatever it was that he was doing, Roger asked: "Have you some men that we could borrow to help force the issue?"

"Certainly, my dear boy! As many as you like. Nothing I like better than a bit of Stanley-bashing. Not these days, anyway!" He slapped my thigh and started coughing all over again.

"The idea was to avoid fighting," I pointed out, rubbing myself where Sir Thomas had landed his playful blow. The trouble with knights, even quite old ones, is that they have no idea of their own strength.

"Hmmm! Devilish tricky!" objected Sir Thomas. "Never understand these subtle policies myself. I was brought up in the old school. Bash the bastards as hard as you can, before they get around to bashing you. My father served Harry the Fifth, you know. Damn fine King. He knew how to bash 'em. Frogs, rebels, anyone who got in his bloody way. Take my word, that's how to do it."

"We have to get the banner back," Roger went on, "and without starting a civil war in the North. My lady is right. We can't go storming Wigan Church with an army. But I don't know what the hell else to do, except go down there and have a look for ourselves. There may be an answer. How far is it to Wigan?"

"Fifteen miles. Maybe less," grunted Pilkington. You could see the disappointment on his face, for all the world like a little boy who'd been promised a sweetmeat and then received only the cat's share of a mackerel. He had obviously been looking forward to cleaning the rust off his battle-axe.

We borrowed one of Pilkington's men to guide us, but it still took us the best part of the day to pick our way through the mosses. There was quite a company of us. Guy had come along, of course, and there was Roger's esquire, Arthur, as well as a couple of yeoman servants, William and Benjamin, or Bill and Ben as we called them. These two were none too bright, but they were built on a similar scale to Roger's destrier, and added no end to our sense of security. Lastly there was my damosel, Juliana. Juliana had a really nice line in complaining and predicting disaster, and, although she came in handy when I needed my gown lacing up or my hair braided, I could have got along without her. However, when one is the wife of a knight banneret one is expected to maintain certain standards, and one was pushing it a bit by making do with only one woman.

Wigan, I have to say, is not the centre of the universe. In essence it's a single street, and not much of a street at that. They had a bit of a market in progress, but to be honest I've seen more business going on in the solar at Middleham.

The church was surrounded by men wearing the Stanley livery. As nasty a bunch of rogues as I have ever seen, and none too anxious to show strangers around. You'd have thought that they had the Holy Grail in there, and the Philosopher's Stone into the bargain. And the title deeds to France.

We put up at the alehouse nearest the church, the *Eagle and Child*. This was a crap hole, but it was the best crap hole in town. The place was named after the Stanley cognizance, by the way, the very badge that was worn on the arm of all those affable gentlemen around the church. Apparently some old Stanley persuaded his wife to adopt his bastard child by leaving it for her to find under an eagle's nest in the garden. The lady, who was barren, and either very clever or very stupid, promptly obliged by taking the baby on board. (I'd have been inclined to shove it up in the nest, if only to see what he did next.)

"There's probably a secret passage from this place to the church," said Roger, gnawing his way through one of the huge pies for which Wigan is famous. "There usually is, so that the priest can nip out for a swift half during Mass. I'll get Master Holt the landlord drunk, and see if I can wheedle the secret out of him."

It was well after midnight before my master came to bed, and he was nothing if not rat-legged after drinking numerous quarts of Holt's beer. He had to hold on to the bed curtains to steady himself while he pissed up the wall. Then he began to tell the bolster how beautiful it was, and how much he wanted it to give him another fine son. I think he only puked about fifteen times. To be honest, I lost count.

When he woke, he sat clutching his head and groaning for about an hour and three-quarters. Then he told me that there was no passage to the church, after all. There had been one in the old days, but the Town Council had sent a man round to condemn it as unsafe, and they'd blocked it up with stones. This was many years ago, when King John was still in nappies, and no one even knew where it had been.

"Brilliant," I said, less than impressed. "I think the only answer is for us to stay here while I embroider a replacement banner. We'll swear blind that it's the original, and no one will be any the wiser. It'll only take about three months."

I don't think that Roger treasured the idea of all those weeks in Wigan. "We could try having a quiet word with Stanley himself," he suggested.

I had to agree that the idea had certain merits. I fancied having a look inside Lathom House. It was odds on that there'd be some interesting papers lying around somewhere. People like Stanley always have a couple of conspiracies on the boil. It gives them something to talk about with their friends.

"A pity I haven't got a letter of authority from the King," he went on. "That'd certainly help him to see sense."

"That's no problem," I said, opening my travelling box and rooting around inside my spare hennin until I found my copy of the Privy Seal.

Roger snatched it from me, staring at the die as if he'd never seen a seal in his life.

"Have you any idea of the penalty for forging the King's seal?" he asked, putting on his Justice-of-the-Peace-for-Gloucestershire voice.

"It's not a forgery, it's a duplicate, and I've full authority to use it in an emergency. If saving the entire North of England from civil war is not an emergency then I don't know what the hell is. Let's get something down on parchment, and then we can get on our way after breakfast."

Don't let the name fool you. Lathom House is a castle, and a hellishly formidable one at that. Getting in to such a place is rarely a problem, it's the getting out that can give you the odd difficulty.

We were politely received by the Steward and shown into lodgings that not even Northumberland would have scorned. The price of the wall hangings alone would have bought half of Scotland. Stanley was not short of a biscuit or two, that was for sure.

Roger and I got out of our clothes, which had more than the odd trace of the local mire on them, and into our Court gear. In a situation like this you have to go out of your way to look as if you've got more money than sense. It helps people to take you seriously. Roger wore his collar of golden Yorkist suns, to show that he was one of the King's knights, ludicrous piked shoes to show that he was fashionable, and a massive codpiece to show that he had a vivid imagination. I wore a top-of-the-range butterfly hennin, with enough wire and gauze to rig a ship of war, and a gown of crimson velvet with a train so long that it saved the Stanleys the trouble of sweeping their floors for the next century.

When we were quite composed we walked down to supper, our attendants forming a suitable procession behind us. We paused at the entrance to the hall, and looked up at the big sign above the doorway. It said:

'*THIS IS LATHOM*

(Maximum hennin room VIII feet, VI inches.)'

"I'm impressed!" snorted Guy, spitting at it.

"Kindly remember, all of you, that we are here as guests," Roger instructed. "I want the absolute minimum of hassle. Understand?"

Some bowing oik with a fancy stick led us up to the top table, where Stanley was sprawled in the biggest chair, picking his teeth with a knife. Next to him was his wife. Lady Margaret Beaufort.

Those of you who have not fallen asleep will remember Lady Margaret from the early part of my story. She had been through another husband since then, Sir Henry Stafford, and was now onto her third, she and Stanley having fallen deeply in love with each other's money.

The process of diplomacy now began. For those of you who don't understand what goes on in such circumstances I should explain that we started by mouthing elaborate courtesies all round, no one meaning a word of it. We did not get down to business. We did not go within a hundred miles of it. We talked about everything else under the sun while we tucked into the feast that had been laid before us.

Roger, to be quite honest, was always very much better than me at this sort of thing. I tend to get bored after about the first three hours of sustained politeness, especially when I'm dealing with people I despise. I really would have made a lousy duchess. If you're married to a royal duke you spend half your life smiling and nodding at ambassadors, mayors, abbots, sheriffs, and other sundry creeps as they try to talk you into twisting your husband's balls on their behalf. (This may sound a crude description of the process, but it's what it amounts to.)

Stanley's men began to clear the lower tables away.

"We're hosting the heats of the All-Lancashire Hoodman Blind Championship tonight," he explained. "Perhaps you'd both care to take part?"

"Not in this hennin," I said hurriedly.

Call me boring if you will, but staggering about with my head in a bag while everyone else beats me has never been my idea of fun.

"Perhaps Dame Beauchamp would prefer to withdraw to see my new manuscript," suggested Lady Margaret, smiling carefully, like a woman with no teeth. Perhaps she thought that there was a tax on opening her mouth too far.

"I should enjoy that more than a multiple orgasm," I replied, inclining my head towards her.

We made our way from the table and up the stairs to Margaret's private solar. This was a cross between a chapel and a library. I'd never seen so many books in one place in my life. I reckon she had at least fifty, and a good half of them were not even in English. She told me that she'd even written one or two of them herself.

She took down the manuscript from the shelf. It turned out to be a family tree, very prettily drawn, of the descendants of King Henry III. That meant that you could find both of us on it for a start, although I didn't consider my portrait to be particularly flattering. Mind you, it got a shade crowded as the generations expanded, with half the people in England above the rank of yeoman. I think the idea was that you could work out where you stood in line to the throne, and how many you needed to kill in order to get there.

I reckoned that if about one hundred and thirty-eight people dropped dead over night I'd become Alianore, Queen of England and of France, of that name the First. Margaret was quite a bit closer, but not as close as she liked everyone to believe.

"Where is your son?" I asked, pointing at his portrait. The artist had obviously never seen Henry Tudor. He had left off the horns and tail. "I noticed he was not in the hall."

"You refer to the Earl of Richmond?" she asked snootily, as if I had just crawled out of the cesspit.

"The only one you've got, isn't he?"

"We do not all breed like conies, Dame Beauchamp. Richmond is in exile. Safer so. Since the death of King Henry and the Prince, my son is the senior surviving Lancastrian claimant."

"Hmmm!" I said, thinking back to a profitable afternoon I had spent in Warwick's library, reading *Every Damosel's Guide to Genealogy*. "I'm none too sure of that. I think you will find that King Henry IV, of unblessed memory, the first of our Lancastrian sovereigns, specifically excluded the Beaufort family from the succession. Even though the Beauforts of the time were his own half-brothers, old John of Gaunt's bastards."

"Legitimated bastards," Margaret returned, somewhat testily. "Henry Bolingbroke had no right to make such a distinction."

"Even so, it does make your son's claim a tad thin. I can't believe that King Edward lies awake at night worrying about it."

You could tell that she didn't want my advice on the subject. She snorted and pulled another book from the shelf. As it opened a letter fell out. I bent to pick it up, but she snatched it from me so fiercely that my fingers almost caught fire. I only had time to see that it was from someone called Morton.

"You know Morton," Roger assured me. "Dr John Morton. Master of the Rolls. Clever fellow. Spends all his time sniffing round for a bishopric. Dare say he'll get one in time. Probably be Chancellor into the bargain. He was a Lancastrian right up to Tewkesbury, but he's too damned useful for the King to bear grudges on that account."

"I'll have to ask Hastings to send his file up," I said. "Margaret Beaufort sure as hell didn't want me to know what he had to say to her, and I'd be interested to know why. How did you get on with Stanley?"

"He's a slippy bastard. It's hard to tie him down. Anyway, at least I'm through to the quarterfinals of the Hoodman Blind tournament."

"Husband," I said, "that is truly a big deal. I come to the regretful conclusion that we are no further on than we were when we bloody started."

I decided that I needed to have a scout around. Next morning Roger and Stanley rode out for a day's hunting, while Margaret went off for one of her long sessions in the chapel. I claimed to be ill, and in need of my bed, but it wasn't long before I was sneaking my way into the Stanleys' private apartments.

There were some interesting papers in there, believe me. Stanley had spent years going from one side to another, like a ferryman, and at times he had had the cheek to ask York and Lancaster to bid against each other for his services! Now, it seemed, he was trying to play King Edward off against Clarence, with Henry Tudor as a spare counter in the background, ready to be brought into the game at any time. At the same time, and despite what she had said to me, his wife was busily intriguing for her son to be allowed home from exile, and it was clear that the man Morton was her agent at Court, greasing palms and issuing threats on her behalf as appropriate.

I was just getting ready to copy down some of the most incriminating bits when in walked Lady Margaret. She drew herself up to her full height. (About four foot.)

"So," she cried triumphantly, "it's as I suspected. You're here to resume your affair with my husband. Why else would you seek out his bedchamber?"

I have to admit that I laughed. "You bloody fool! I'd not go with Lord Stanley if each drop of his body fluid came complete with a free manor house in Kent. Give me some credit for taste."

"There were rumours at Court."

"They were someone's idea of a joke. Mine, in fact."

"Then what are you doing here?" Her eyes went to the pile of letters and other documents on the bed and she had her answer. She was carrying a breviary in her hand to show how religious she was. Now she slid a nasty little dagger out of its spine and advanced on me.

I snatched my hennin off. Inside I had something similar but even nastier, supplied by Hastings, an Italian job as used in the best murders in Milan. It had a fancy little knob in the crosspiece that sent a second blade shooting out of the hilt. Just the job for slicing pears.

She lunged at me. It's at times like this when you wish that you weren't wearing skirts. They don't half get in the way when you're dodging a knife, and the only saving grace was that she was similarly encumbered. I tripped her as she flew past me, and she struck her nut on the chamber-pot with a clang that they probably heard back in Middleham.

"You'd better put that down before you get hurt," I said. "I'm bigger and stronger than you, and I've won more fights than you've had syllabubs."

She stood up, shaking the pain out of her head, then raised the dagger again and started to circle around me, working herself up to strike.

"You're still in my castle," she said, "and you are not going to escape. I'm going to call for help. We'll soon see who has the advantage here."

"I'd have a look behind you first," I suggested.

She grinned at me.

"Really, Alianore! I expected better than that from you. That trick is so old that you couldn't catch Julius Caesar with it!"

She was still grinning when Guy dropped the big sack over her head and twisted the knife out of her hand. Well, I did warn her.

"Well done, Guy!" I said.

"All in a day's work, my lady."

"You know what to do? Plan C?"

"Doddle, my lady. Do it with our eyes closed. Won't we, lads?"

Bill and Ben walked in, grinning inanely. Between them they tied Margaret up so tightly that she couldn't even wrinkle her nose. Then they wrapped her up in the carpet and carried her out of the castle.

Where, I hear you ask, were her legion of damosels, her esquires, her pages, her gentlemen of the household? Well, I don't really know, although a fair few of them were out hunting with Stanley and Roger. The rest presumably thought that she was disposing of an old carpet and that Guy and the others were taking it to its new home. It's amazing what you can get away with if you've got barefaced cheek. Ask any thief.

That evening we were all about to tuck into our wild boar pottage when an arrow came flying in through a window and buried itself in the table in front of Stanley. (Don't ask me how Guy contrived this without killing anyone, but I like to think that he practised a few times beforehand.)

Stanley dropped his spoon in his pottage, and hot brown liquid flew up into his face. He swore a couple of times and plucked the note from the shaft of the arrow. Everyone within six feet, including me, craned to see what it said. And what it said was:

"If you would see your Lady dear,

Come and seek in Martin Mere.

Bert Amend-All."

It was at this moment that Stanley realised that Margaret was missing. His mouth dropped open, and he stared at the empty place next to him, as if she had just disappeared in a cloud of smoke.

"Martin Mere?" he choked. "A man could catch his death wading about in that morass! I'm damned if I'm going there at this time of night. Damned if I'm going to pay any ransom, either. The buggers can keep her."

Roger was genuinely shocked. "That's unthinkable!" he cried. "You'd lose all respect, all honour. You've no choice but to do as they ask."

"Absolutely," I agreed. "It's not the sort of thing a man in your position can let pass, someone just wandering into your castle in broad daylight and stealing your lady. They might come back tomorrow for the valuables. No, you'll have to summon every man you can muster to avenge this insult."

"An insult, is it?" asked Stanley, thoughtfully.

"I rather think so. Don't you?"

"Happen you're right. We'll have to do summat." He took off his velvet hat, and scratched his bald head in bewilderment. "First thing in the morning. No use crashing about in the dark. That'd do nowt but scare the ducks."

Roger was not best pleased by my choice of tactics when I explained them to him. I suppose I should have acted like a real lady and allowed Margaret Beaufort to stab me to death. As I told him, I'd not set out with the idea of kidnapping her. It just so happened that I'd been forced to implement a contingency plan.

"Where is Lady Margaret now?" he demanded.

"On her way to Wigan with Guy and Bill."

"And what are you going to do with her?"

"I haven't quite worked that bit out."

"Alianore, have you any idea how bloody dangerous this is? Margaret Beaufort is well in at Court. She and the Queen are like that." He twisted one finger around another. "If Stanley finds out that we're behind this, it won't just be him that we have to deal with. It'll be the King himself."

I smiled at him. "I've got my hands on some very tasty letters and papers, and if old Stanley tries to give us any aggravation I'll pay Caxton to make a book of them. That'll settle his hash, as they say in Yorkshire."

"The kidnapping of noble ladies is strictly forbidden by the Knightly Code," my husband went on, still annoyed with me. "I could get a six month suspension from jousting for this."

"Roger," I answered patiently, "we are living in the late fifteenth century. Modern times. No one gives a toss any more about knightly codes or the rest of that old crap. It's all about power politics and ruthless ambition nowadays. We make up the rules as we go along."

He frowned at me and pulled out his copy of the Code. It had belonged to his great-grandfather and was all neatly copied out and illustrated by a monk, too, none of your cheap, modern, printed rubbish. On the title page was a picture of Edward III picking up the Countess of Salisbury's garter. (This incident led to the founding of the Order of the Garter, with its famous motto *Honi Soit Qui Mal Y Pense*, which can be translated as *Just Because A Woman's Garter Falls Down It Doesn't Mean That The King Is Bonking Her*.)

"Look," Roger cried, stabbing his finger into the thing, "paragraph eighteen: 'No knight, esquire, or armiger shall carry off, ravish or imprison any lady, damosel or gentlewoman (except for the purpose of taking her in canonical marriage against her will) under pain of six months banishment from all tournaments in Western Europe and a fine of twenty-four shillings.'"

"Like I said, it's just a load of old manure," I snorted. "If King Arthur has a vacancy I dare say he'll send for you, but until then you'll just have to live in the real world with the rest of us."

"There are certain things that are sacred, Alianore, and knightly vows are among them. The Code is all that distinguishes us from barbarians and savages. It obliges the strong to protect the weak. Above all it safeguards children, and honours all ladies and gentlewomen." He flicked over a few more pages. "Ah, here it is. I thought it was compulsory in a case of this kind. I'm sorry, my dear, but I'm not allowed to offer you an alternative."

He grabbed me, pulled me down across his thighs, and began to bunch my skirts up around my waist.

"What the hell are you doing?" I asked.

"Correcting my wife in accordance with paragraph twenty-two," he said, landing the first slap squarely across my bare bum. "It instructs me to do this to any lady under my protection who mocks the Knightly Code. It's a matter of duty."

"I could cope with you being a little less dutiful," I protested, somewhat breathlessly.

"I do apologise, beloved," he said, landing another spank, "but I can't possibly infringe the Code twice in one day. I'm not enjoying this, you know."

"Bloody liar!" I said. "Ouch!"

Stanley and his shower spent the whole of the next day wading around Martin Mere, which is the biggest, wettest marsh in a very large and very wet marshy area. Finding nothing except the secret of collecting slime in their boots they came home in a very merry mood. This is what I surmise. By the time they returned to Lathom we were a very long way along our road.

We passed quite a few of Stanley's followers along the way, and it was no surprise to find that his retainers had been withdrawn from around Wigan Church. I expect he sent a scurrier off at first light to collect them. For one reason and another Roger and I were not out of bed quite that early.

Guy had kept Margaret hidden overnight in a convenient cowshed, a most appropriate lodging for her in my opinion.

I had her placed on top of one of the tombs in the church, next to the effigy of a local knight who'd got himself killed at Crecy, or Agincourt, or some other little squabble with the French. I admit that it was not a very appropriate thing to do. The poor man had not done me any harm, after all, and it was wrong of me to lumber him with such an unpleasant companion, even on a temporary basis.

Just before we left I removed her gag. I didn't want to go without giving her a chance to say goodbye.

"You'll pay for this," she spat out.

"What a very original threat," I said. "I'd be completely terrified if I didn't have the whole of your husband's treasonable correspondence in my saddlebag. Any trouble from either of you in future and it'll go straight to Cousin Edward with a nice red ribbon round it. There's nothing the King loves more than a good read, you know."

Margaret said some very rude things after that. Coming from someone with a major reputation for piety it was really quite shocking. Roger had to ask me what some of the words meant, so you can tell how bad it was.

What more is there to tell? We took Gloucester's banner down from where it had been lodged in the chancel and then headed for the hills. By the time Lord and Lady Stanley were able to put all the pieces together we were safely back at Middleham.

Richard was well made up, and I dare say that he'd have knighted Roger all over again if this had been possible. As it was we had to be satisfied with shooting up several places in the league of favour.

I felt that I deserved a somewhat more tangible reward after all that I'd been through, and so I dipped into the Intelligence Fund and treated myself to a new gown of blue sarsenet and a jewelled collar.

The upshot of this adventure was that the Stanley family gave Cousin Richard no further annoyance for several years.

The second upshot was that I never again mocked the Knightly Code in Roger's hearing. Except on his birthday.

VII

Anne bore her husband a fine son, Edward. This was quite an event in the history of the world, as it provoked Richard of Gloucester into a smile. He and Anne now indulged in a kind of perennial honeymoon, ignoring public business so that they could gaze into each other's eyes. Riding off on their own up Coverdale to enjoy the scenery and the fresh air. Exchanging roses they had snapped off in the pleasance. Quite sickening, really. I felt like reminding them that they were living in Yorkshire, not flaming Camelot.

The years slipped by. I am inclined to skip a few of them. We tried to have a war with France, but decided not to bother, much to Gloucester's disgust. Then George Clarence got himself involved in a treason too far.

George never struck me as the romantic type, but the fact remains that he went to pieces after his wife's death. He refused to believe that Isabel had come to a natural end. He swore that the Woodvilles had poisoned her, and the son she had just borne. He had two of her servants hanged to make the point.

It's true that the Queen had some relatives who didn't have enough breeding to be the scum of the earth, men who would cheerfully have sold their own grandmothers for half a groat, but I doubt very much whether George's suspicions were justified. There was no profit for anyone in killing Isabel.

Clarence continued to spout various forms of nonsense, until Cousin Edward decided that enough was enough and had him thrown in the Tower.

At this point Richard did something very unusual. He took his whole household down to the King's Court. Anne included. Me included. He didn't give us much of a briefing on his intentions, but you could tell that he wasn't pleased with the course of events. His face was enough to stop a clock in the next parish.

"Do you know," I said to Cousin Edward, "this business of Clarence is doing nothing for your ratings in the North. In fact, they've plummeted to their lowest levels since 1469. I don't think you can afford all this bad publicity."

We were dancing in the Great Hall at Eltham. It was my first time at Court for ages, and I was desperate to give the King some direct feedback, instead of having my reports filtered as usual by Hastings and the other toads around him. Unfortunately, Edward always hated mixing business with pleasure. In fact, he had grown so lazy that he didn't much care to mix business with anything. He frowned at me angrily.

"Richard's put you up to this I suppose?" he demanded.

"No. But he doesn't like it one bit."

"That's his hard cheddar. George is up to his neck in treason again, and I'm sick of forgiving him. He's already had more chances than Soft Mick."

"Even so," I said, "I consider it my duty to advise you that the people of the North do not take kindly to kings who execute their own brothers. We obtained a very strong negative response to that scenario."

"Look, Alianore," he replied, sighing, "it's time you gave this intelligence lark up and took up some useful occupation. Come back to Court. I've a vacancy for another mistress, and your name was mentioned by the head-hunters."

"Was it indeed? So you've grown weary of Mistress Shore?"

He shook his head. "Mistress Shore is fine when I'm in the mood for her. Cockney high spirits don't always appeal. When I'm in a sad or contemplative humour I turn to another lady who is pious and discreet, and likes to take the lead in bed. The vacancy is for a wise and witty woman who can lift me when it all gets too much. Someone with a few new ideas. You've no idea how incredibly tedious it is to rule England between battles."

"How many mistresses do you have, in point of fact?" I asked.

"A permanent establishment of three. Currently with one vacancy. I'm not completely faithful, of course. I do have the occasional fling outside the regular circle. Sometimes I even have a night with the Queen. But other than that I'm virtually celibate. There's a fellow who looks a bit like me who chases through London, banging away at the citizen's wives. I get blamed for a lot of his work. Used to annoy me until I found out that the Londoners think it's great to have a king who goes around in disguise, screwing their womenfolk. Strange people, the merchants, but they're the ones with all the brass these days, and if that's what they want it's fine by me."

"You forget that I have a husband," I said. I gasped as well, because he had trod on my foot. It made me realise how much weight he'd put on.

"No, I don't. Husbands are usually quite co-operative in these circumstances. It's all very discreet. You don't know the name of my pious lady, do you? And you're a senior operative in Yorkist Intelligence. No one needs know your identity either. You could go under a false name on the mistresses' roster. You'll enjoy the work, and it's extremely well paid."

"Roger is a tad old-fashioned," I replied, shaking my head. "He still believes in the Knightly Code. If I took up your offer he might just throw off his allegiance or something silly like that. I really don't think it's on, you know."

"Ah, well," he sighed, "it was only a thought. I had the idea that you might appreciate a bit of promotion, that's all. Didn't realise that Roger was such a bore."

"The truth is that I'd prefer to retire altogether. Go home to Horton Beauchamp and concentrate on growing gillyflowers and sewing altar cloths. I've always wanted to be ordinary, like my sisters, and instead I'm lumbered with all this high-powered political crap and Court intrigue."

Edward shrugged. "I always fancied the idea of running an alehouse in Stamford. We can't have everything in this life, Alianore."

I asked Hastings for some background on the Clarence business, because no one, so far, had explained the exact nature of George's treason. He cleared his throat noisily, and shuffled the papers on his desk, looking at me as if I had just invited him to castrate himself with a blunt knife.

"The less you know about it, the better," he said, mysteriously.

"What do you mean by that?"

"I don't know half the facts myself. I don't want to know. When the King decides to kill his own brother it makes sense for the rest of us to keep our noses out. Well out."

"And what am I to tell Gloucester?"

"Nothing. There's nothing to tell. Clarence hasn't been dealt with through this Department. It's been a freelance job. The Woodvilles. They collected all the dirt on him. Edward wanted it that way. More to the point, the Queen wanted it that way. Remember that Clarence and Warwick had her father taken out. She's not forgotten that."

"Do you mean that we've had bloody amateurs on the case? And that Clarence is to die on their say-so?"

"I mean exactly that." Hastings leaned back, his hands supporting his head as if he expected it to drop off. His eyes left me to stare at the naked lady depicted on the tapestry behind me, who was doing something very interesting with a snake. "Look, you're not among your Yorkshire wool-brains now. This is the Court. Things are so sophisticated here that even I don't know what's going on half the time. The King is growing fat and idle. The Queen and the Woodvilles are getting to the point where they're virtually running the show. Gloucester might be able to do something about it, if he lowered himself enough to live down here on a regular basis. He prefers to go on chasing sheep in the North. He can't have it all ways."

"I see. And I'm to tell him that?"

"If you like. But don't get any further involved. I don't think you realise what you're up against."

Hastings was not much more forthcoming when I asked him the name of the King's pious mistress.

"You do not need to know that, Alianore," he pronounced, sounding disappointed with me. "The King likes to keep his private life to himself. Especially where ladies of rank are involved. If you want the full amazing truth you'll have to go on the rota yourself. I wish you would. I need someone I can trust in Edward's bed. The present team are all the Queen's creatures."

"There are limits to what I will do for the House of York," I answered huffily. "Having twenty stones of sovereign on top of me on a regular basis is well outside those parameters."

"Then take my advice, and don't poke into matters that don't concern you. And as for the Clarence business, don't touch it with a lance."

I've always known when to take a warning. I kept my mouth shut. It wasn't long before George was found mysteriously upended in a barrel of malmsey in the Tower. The Woodvilles were blamed, not least by Richard, but it was King Edward who gave the order.

Richard was grimmer than ever after that, and swore that he would one day have his revenge on the Queen and her affinity. I'm not sure how much he loved Clarence – they always seemed at daggers drawn to me – but that was not the point. The killing touched on his sense of family honour. It also set an uncomfortable precedent.

More water flowed under the bridges. Richard continued his task of bringing peace and justice to the North, and became quite unreasonably popular. We indulged in sundry quarrels with Scotland, and eventually won back possession of Berwick. Not that Berwick is worth having, of course. Like Calais it costs more to keep than it brings in, but it's a symbol of our English pride. Or our English stupidity.

I had little part in all this. The life of a knight's lady can be seriously dull. It isn't all repelling sieges and being carried off by black-hearted villains, you know. Even when you're deeply involved in intelligence work, you still spend a lot of time keeping the children quiet, mending shirts, receiving boring guests and trying to make sense of account rolls.

I suppose I could tell you more about our life in Gloucestershire, but a description of my herb garden at Horton Beauchamp would be unlikely to set your feet twitching. We had quarrels with our neighbours, of course, but who hasn't? Nothing much came of them in the end. The dispute with the monks of Cirencester over grazing rights raised a few hairs at the time, but the plain fact is that the Abbot recovered perfectly well from his night roaming the high tops of the Cotswolds without his clothes. I hear that it was only a very bad cold that he caught, and definitely not pneumonia. In any case, Bill and Ben misunderstood their orders, and they did apologise rather nicely. So you see it was nothing to do with me at all.

No, if you want to read about quarrels with the neighbours I suggest you ask John Paston to lend you his family's collection of letters. He's put them all in a box, and plans to keep them for future generations. Though I cannot imagine why he thinks that posterity will be interested in his sister's affair with Richard Calle, his brother's collection of seedy little friends, or the price of corn in Norfolk in the twentieth year of Mad Harry's reign.

Paston's a damned lawyer, of course, like the rest of his tribe. No trade for a gentleman, that. The obnoxious little Tudor Slimebag positively encourages Paston and his like, men who use the law as a means of lining their pockets instead of stealing by force of arms like honest folk. This proves that he, Tudor, or Tydder, or whatever the hell he calls himself, is no gentleman either.

I'm sorry to say that one of my nephews lowered himself sufficiently to marry Paston's sister-in-law, and so I have to admit to having JP (as he signs himself) in the family. It must be a chilly day in hell when someone like me, directly descended from Alfred of Wessex, William the Bastard, King Edward III, El Cid, the Fair Maid of Kent and Sir James of Audley, the hero of Poitiers, has to acknowledge kinship with a man whose great-great-grandfather was a serf, and fondly imagines that the people of the distant future will want to read his laundry list. However, that's the way things are these days. Country's gone completely to the dogs since Bosworth, mark my words.

I have strayed from my point. Forgive me. Let's go back to Middleham. (Though thankfully only in our minds.) The fact is that nothing much happened there.

I was just in the middle of composing a very delicate letter to the Earl of Angus, a small contribution to our continuing attempts to make life difficult for James III of Scotland, when the messenger from Hastings arrived. Richard and Anne were up in Coverdale, hunting, with most of the household around them. It would be an exaggeration to say that I was left in charge of the castle, but not much of one.

I'd been expecting a briefing letter from Hastings for some time, but noticed at once that this one was unusually thick.

Moreover, there was another plump letter for Gloucester himself. Something was very wrong.

"Why are you in black?" I asked the messenger, Will Catesby.

"The King is dead, my lady," he got out, still choking from the dust.

"It's sure?" I asked, astonished. "He really is dead?"

Catesby nodded. "They were half way through embalming him when I left London, so he better had be."

"Did you come by way of York?"

"Yes, my lady."

"Are the tidings known there?"

"I said nothing, my lady, but I dare say that the merchants will soon pick it up through their own channels. As you know, this sort of thing has an impact on commercial confidence, and will lead to significant movements in the market."

I nodded. "Await the Duke, Catesby. Give him his letter. Apart from that, keep your mouth closed. I don't want him getting the idea that anyone here was told before he was. Understand?"

He did. William Catesby always understood the need for silence. He'd not become one of Hastings' top agents by accident. His only fault was that he was yet another damned lawyer.

I wept for Cousin Edward, being the sentimental fool that I am, and then hurried to the chapel to pray for his soul. This duty done, I summoned my husband's esquire, Arthur, and gave him the entire Intelligence Fund, three rings from my fingers, Constance's christening cup and thirteen pounds six shillings and four pence from Roger's spare purse.

"Go to York," I said. "Go directly to York. Do not pause at the alehouse. Do not seek out damosels in distress. Buy up every ell of black cloth in the place."

The money I made from that deal paid for a whole lot of wainscoting back at Horton Beauchamp.

Edward's elder son, also Edward, was now King Edward the Fifth. He was only twelve years old and so he needed a Protector to manage the business for him. Richard was the obvious choice for the job, but Queen Elizabeth Woodville did not see it that way. She tried to fiddle matters so that her boy was crowned before Gloucester even heard of his brother's death. Hastings had put paid to that notion by sending Richard warning of her intentions.

Richard rode south, caught up with the young King at Stony Stratford, took him into care, and despatched sundry Woodvilles to prison. I can't give you the full details, because Anne and I were not invited to this particular party, but according to Roger it wasn't necessary to strike a single blow.

The Queen fled into sanctuary, taking the rest of her children with her. A trusting sort, Elizabeth Woodville.

I arrived in London on 5th June, a Thursday it was, with Anne and the rest of her ladies. Anne did not appreciate the change of scene one bit. It didn't help that she'd been forced to leave her son behind at Middleham. He was a sickly boy, and she didn't fancy exposing him to the unhealthy stinks of London in summer, which often breed plague and other diseases in the weak.

"I've always hated the Court, Alianore," she confided. "I know Richard had no choice, but I do wish he could have turned this job down. He's a soldier, not a politician, and one way or another the bastards down here will make mincemeat of him."

It seemed to me that it would certainly be necessary to take one or two people out of the game before we could all sleep soundly in our beds again. However, I'll not pretend that I was sorry to see the back of Middleham. In fact I was quite looking forward to dancing at Court, going to all the best tournaments and wearing fashionable clothes again. Moreover, it looked like a good opportunity to give up my intelligence work and settle down to the easy life of a lady-in-waiting, carrying Anne's train from time to time or writing the odd letter on her behalf. At last I'd be able to fulfil my lifelong ambition to be an ordinary woman, instead of being up to my neck in boring old power politics.

We lodged at Baynards Castle, which belonged to Richard's mother. It was Monday, and I was still busy helping Anne to unpack when William Catesby put his ferret face around the door. I thought that it was another briefing from Hastings, but it turned out to be a lot more serious than that.

"Can you get me in to see Gloucester?" he asked.

"He's a tad busy at the moment. Waiting time is at least a week for anyone below the rank of earl or archbishop. Even the Duchess only gets to see him in bed. You should go through the channels. Lord Lovel's your man, he keeps the appointment diary."

"This is an intelligence matter, Dame Beauchamp. Top secret."

"You can tell me. I've been positively vetted."

"So has Hastings," he muttered. "Look, I know you're part of Yorkist Intelligence, but this matter is so sensitive, so extraordinarily dangerous, that I daren't breathe a word to anyone but the Protector himself. Nothing personal, you understand. It's just that I can't take the risk."

"All right," I said, "I'll see what I can do. Just step this way."

We climbed stairs and walked along passages for a good five minutes until we reached the room that Gloucester was using for his Council chamber. Two enormous Yorkshire lads armed with billhooks were guarding the door, but they stood out of my way.

Richard was sitting at a big table, with Francis Lovel and some foppish fellow I didn't recognise. The three of them were almost buried under a mound of papers. He glanced up as the door opened, and I saw at once that I was about as welcome as a wet dog in a bridal bed.

"Your Grace, I have to give you an urgent security briefing," I announced.

"That's a new name for it!" snorted the fop, laughing crudely. I saved time by taking an instant dislike to him and to his disgusting taste in clothes. Never trust any man who dresses in violet silk, that's my counsel.

"Is there no end to your witty jests, Cousin Buckingham?" Richard asked. To my amazement he was more or less chuckling.

I had heard a lot about Buckingham since my arrival in London, mostly complaints about his growing influence, but this was my first sight of him. He'd been living under a stone during King Edward's reign, and had just crawled out.

"Is the matter really so urgent?" Richard asked me.

"Vitally so."

"Then speak out. There's nothing that can't be said in front of my Cousin Buckingham."

I frowned. I'd have liked to have gone away and checked my files first, because I had a funny feeling that Buckingham wasn't even entitled to know how many barrels of ale the Chancery clerks could shift in a year. He was closely related to Margaret Beaufort, and there was a distinct smell of Lancastrian about him. He was married to one of the Queen's sisters, but despite that Cousin Edward had never given him so much as a day's work, and Cousin Edward, for all his faults, was always a shrewd judge.

Before I could open my mouth again, Catesby opened his. I don't know what I'd expected, but it was certainly not a patch on what came out. Hastings was organising a conspiracy against the Protector. Hastings! And to make it even more amazing he had gone into league with the Queen, the Woodvilles, the Archbishop of York, Mistress Shore and Bishop Morton of Ely.

I was seriously worried. It looked very much as if I'd enabled a madman to waste Richard's valuable time with a load of crap. Hastings was a randy old goat who couldn't keep his hands to himself, but he'd been a loyal Yorkist all his life, and he hated the Queen and the Woodvilles. Moreover, as you'll remember, it was Hastings who'd enabled Richard to thwart the Woodvilles in the first place. What reason was there for him to change sides at this stage?

"Why would Hastings do this?" Richard demanded, as if reading my thoughts.

"Because he believes that Your Grace intends to usurp the throne," Catesby answered. "He has sworn to prevent it."

"Hastings has taken the Shore woman under his roof, I hear," sneered Buckingham. "She's always been the Queen's creature, and doubtless has her ways of winning a man around."

Gloucester's face twisted with disgust. He never did like to think of people enjoying themselves too much, especially where a bed was involved. It was one of his little quirks. "Foul whore!" he spat out. "It was she, and those like her, who brought my brother low. And Hastings was Edward's pimp for years."

"Time for reinforcements," suggested Lovel.

"Yes, Francis. We'll mobilise the North, and crush this conspiracy."

"Scant time for that," said Buckingham. "Send for the soldiers, yes. No problem with that. But Hastings needs to have an accident with an axe. Straightaway. Dead men give very little hassle."

"We'll get him on Friday, at the Council meeting," said Richard briskly. "Dame Beauchamp, you'll use the interim to gather further evidence. I want a result. I want these bastards nailed to the wall."

"Hang on," Buckingham put in. "This woman has been working for Hastings for years. Am I right? Eh? Or am I right? Are you sure you can trust her not to leak this?"

"Now just listen here, you walking bag of puke," I said, mildly irritated by his tone, "I don't know where you've been for the last fifteen years or so, but I've risked my life for the House of York more times than you've kissed your wife's Woodville arse. Accuse me of treason again and you'll need to go out shopping for a new face."

"Thank you for sharing that with us, Alianore," Richard said, soothingly. "We're all friends here. Harry was just pointing out that you've got links with Hastings as well as with me. It's true enough, but I trust you to get on with the job."

Fortified by this vote of confidence, I shot off to Westminster to have a flick through Buckingham's security file. What I found in there set my knees trembling. To describe Cousin Harry as politically unreliable was a bit like saying that Clarence used to treat himself to the odd glass of malmsey on special occasions.

I took this evidence back to Baynards Castle, so that Richard could have something to read in bed. This was a complete waste of time. For some reason that I shall never be able to explain if I live to be sixty, Buckingham was confused in his mind with St Francis of Assisi. He just would not believe anything bad of him. This was part of the problem with Hastings, whose nose had been put well out of joint by the growth of Buckingham's influence.

I went on with my investigations. I had Guy follow Mistress Shore, a task that he enjoyed no end, and she led him by a devious route from Hastings' house, to Morton's place in Holborn and on to Westminster Sanctuary and then all the way back again. The journey was repeated the next day, and the next, but on the third occasion she met up with an unpleasant gang of foot pads with Yorkshire accents, and the letters she was carrying went off for a little walk of their own.

They were in code, but it was a simple variation of our standard Intelligence cipher, and by staying up overnight I had it cracked by early on Friday morning. I tidied myself up a little and went downstairs to the solar, where Anne was tucking into a large plate of strawberries.

"Delicious!" she cried, beaming. "Try one, Alianore. They're a present from Bishop Morton."

"Morton!" I repeated dozily. "From Morton? For Christ's sake, leave them alone! It's shorter than even money that they're poisoned!"

I hurried across, and snatched a strawberry literally out of her mouth. She turned white.

"I've already had three," she admitted. "Richard, old greedy-guts, has had the best part of a dozen. Oh, God! Where is he?"

We found Gloucester in the garderobe, with it coming out of him at both ends. I hurried off to get the herbs out, mixed a Tegolin special, and then poured it down their throats. Anne got away more or less scot-free as a result, apart from being sick a couple of times, but Richard was in quite a bad way. Although not nearly in such a state as he'd have been if I'd not got the antidote into him in time. He spent much of the rest of the day running off to the privy, which caused certain complications during the Council meeting at the Tower, as you shall see.

VIII

The Council meeting.

I was not entitled to be present, of course, but Richard made special arrangements for me to be accommodated in a tiny gallery, high in the wall of the room, which had obviously been put in to allow some crafty king to overhear what his Council had to say when he was supposedly somewhere else. The style of the architecture made me think that it was probably the first Edward. Anyway, the point is that from this gallery you could hear and see everything going on below and, unless you really leaned forward and shouted, there was no chance of anyone downstairs spotting your presence.

Buckingham was one of the first to arrive, with old Jocky Howard. Then the Archbishop of York, Rotherham, showed up, thin as a lath, wearing an expression that made you feel he grudged you the air you breathed. Stanley was next. I'd not been able to tie him into the conspiracy, which was a blow bearing in mind his wife's known links with Morton. He started to tell the others about some nightmare he had had, involving a bore who had razed an elm, but no one was interested.

(Some people will tell you that Stanley was involved in the Hastings conspiracy. This is a lie. He had history rewritten later on in an attempt to prove himself a long-term supporter of Henry Tudor. The truth is that at this point he was backing Richard to the hilt. He always was good at choosing the winning side. Richard was later to make him Constable of England, which he most certainly would not have done if Stanley had already committed overt treason. Richard made his mistakes, but he wasn't a complete idiot.)

Morton rolled in next. A gross, shifty looking fellow with deep-set eyes, unimpressive to look at but as clever a rogue as has ever been born. It is of course he who, in late years, has devised the method of taxation known as Morton's Fork. By this, a man who is obviously rich is judged to be well able to afford to cough up for the King. A man who appears to be poor is assumed to have money hidden away somewhere, and so is equally eligible to pay. Hence the expression: 'Fork off, Morton'.

Hastings arrived. He looked cheerful, and greeted his colleagues as if they all owed him money and were proposing to pay it back immediately with double interest. He started to tell Buckingham what he'd been up to the previous night with Mistress Shore, doubtless trying to make him jealous.

"It's getting on the late side," said Stanley, interrupting. "Must be near on five-and-twenty to nine. Where's Gloucester? Still abed?"

"A bit rough," Buckingham answered. "Too much London ale. Eh?"

One or two of them forced a laugh. Powerful men can always make people chuckle, even when they're not so much wits as half-wits. Buckingham could have earned a living on any stage. They always need someone to sweep up.

It was after nine before Richard arrived, bringing with him Francis Lovel and Will Catesby. It's ironic, but a fact, that Catesby had been put on the Council at Hastings' recommendation. Trust none but 'theesen', as they say in Yorkshire.

Richard looked poorly. There's no other word for it. He sat down, but he was restless, uncomfortable, almost squirming in his place. They had just got about half way through the minutes of the last meeting when he stood up, clutching his belly.

"My lord," he said to Morton, "you've some right good strawberries in your garden at Holborn. Let's have a mess of them. Nothing like a strawberry to settle the stomach."

Gloucester knew how to dig. I thought I saw Morton flinch, but if he did it was only for an instant. The man was always a real professional, I'll grant him that. He wobbled to the door, called for his boy, and sent the lad off on the errand.

Richard had no sooner resumed business than he had to halt it again. He was away for a good hour, and when he came back again I could see that he was just about holding himself together. He sat in silence, twisting his rings, his face white. He was so unlike himself that even Hastings realised that something was wrong.

"Are you ill, Richard?" he asked.

Gloucester flared up. He was, after all, in quite a bit of pain. He punched the table with his fist.

"What have they deserved," he demanded, "that compass and imagine the destruction of me, being so near in blood unto the King, and the Protector of his royal person?"

"Death," said Hastings, as much out of habit, I think, as anything else.

"Whoever they may be?"

"Absolutely."

"That sorceress, my brother's wife, and the Shore witch, and others with them, have wrought this on my body."

He rolled back his left sleeve, and showed the blotches left on his skin by the poison. It was clever of Richard to blame it on sorcery. It's always very difficult to prove deliberate poisoning. Of course it's also difficult to prove sorcery, but the point is that you don't need to bother. The accusation is usually enough.

You could see that Hastings was worried, and for the first time. He'd not exactly made a state secret of the fact that he'd spent the previous night rolling around in Elizabeth Shore's bed. Buckingham grinned, and winked at him.

"If they have done this …" began Hastings.

"If?" bawled Richard. "If? Bugger the ifs! Look at my arm. Look at it, traitor!"

He hammered the table again, and this time the signal worked. The door flew open, and armed men flooded into the room. Roger was in the forefront, with Thomas Howard, James Tyrell, and Rob Percy. I noticed that Roger's war-hammer accidentally smacked into Stanley's face, with the result that Stanley ended up under the table, his nose spouting blood, but this was not at all intentional. Not at all.

From where I was sitting it was as good as a play.

"Hastings, you are arrested," said Gloucester. I had never heard his voice grow so cold. "I swear I'll not dine until your head is off."

I thought that this was a figure of speech, but it wasn't. Richard had him taken outside and beheaded on a pile of logs, without further ado. Morton and Archbishop Rotherham, being clergymen, could only be locked up, and they were.

This was Richard's first big mistake. He should have given Hastings a trial, if only for the look of the thing. He should have questioned him in depth, if only to get to the bottom of the conspiracy. He should, moreover, have arranged for Morton to have a tragic accident. I told him all this later, but by then it was too late. He sighed wearily, like a man being nagged by his wife, and made me Acting Head of Yorkist Intelligence.

"And what's to stop them trying again?" asked Anne.

I stared at her, surprised. There was quite a crowd of us gathered in the solar at Crosby Place, and her loud question turned many heads besides mine.

"The King will not be a boy forever," she went on. "He's a Woodville, through and through, everyone knows that. In a few years he'll be after his revenge. My lord, he will do to you what his family did to Clarence. What will happen to our son? And your other children?"

Richard looked uncomfortable. He sat twiddling with his rings as he tried to come up with a good answer. The trouble was, he couldn't think of one. "What would you have me do?"

"Take the crown. It's the only way to be safe."

"Anne is right," said Buckingham, loudly. He stood there, tossing his head, as if he wanted to be sure that everyone was watching him. They were. "It won't just be you and your son. If the Woodville shower get back in the saddle it'll be the whole lot of us."

"And what possible pretext can I use to justify such treachery? Tell me that."

"There's the old tale that your brother was a bastard, the son of the archer, Blaeburn," Buckingham replied. He was so pat with it that I knew at once that it was his favourite fairy story.

"Have you met my mother?" Richard asked, icily. "Half an hour with her and you'd know better than to come up with such rubbish."

"It's amazing what you can get people to believe," Buckingham said. "It doesn't matter whether it's true or not, as long as people believe it."

He laughed, and it was not a moment for laughing. I saw a new light in Richard's eye; for the first time he doubted him.

"Surely," said Anne, "there is something in those files of yours that would soothe my lord's conscience."

I was helping her to undress. She had sent the rest of her women away, a most unusual occurrence, and so I had guessed what was coming.

"The Duchess of York has one of the thinnest security records in Westminster," I answered. "She has never put a foot wrong in her life. For the last twenty-odd years she's lived like a nun, saying more prayers in a day than you or I do in a year. The tale of Blaeburn was very thoroughly investigated by Hastings, on King Edward's own orders, and found to be utterly groundless, a vile Lancastrian smear."

"And yet Richard is said to resemble the Duke of York, his father, as Edward and Clarence never did. I remember my father remarking on it."

"Children don't always look like their fathers," I objected, bearing in mind two of my own, "and in any event, I can't see Richard dishing the dirt on his own mother. It's not his style."

"There may be another tack," she suggested. "My father and Clarence seemed to think that there was something iffy about Edward's marriage to Elizabeth. Some impediment, I mean. I don't know what, but it might be worth a look."

"They were certainly married in secret," I said, "and that's always suspicious. But don't build your hopes up. It's short odds that anything really meaty in the way of proof will have been sent floating down the Thames years ago."

"We can always try a bit of fabrication, Alianore."

It was easy to forget that Anne was Warwick the Kingmaker's daughter. She had just made a very good job of reminding me.

"Have you thought this through?" I asked. "If Richard does become King you'll be stuck at Court for the rest of your days. No more Middleham. You'll be lucky to get north of Luton."

"I know. But it's Richard's life, and my son's life. I'll do anything to save them. If I have to become Queen, and spend the rest of my life within twenty-five miles of London, then that's just the way it's got to be. We all have to make sacrifices for England."

I was at my desk well before Prime next morning, and started ploughing through the archives. I sensed that it was going to be a long day, with nothing to show at the end of it. Some people believe that all the secrets of the world can be found in the government's intelligence files, but I can assure you that much of the documentation is practically useless, except as a means of collecting dust, and the indexing system leaves a great deal to be desired. There was nothing at all under, *Marriage, King Edward IV*, although surprisingly I did find a slim file listed under, *Sorcery, Woodville, E.*

Roger dropped in just before noon to take me into London for dinner at his favourite cook-shop. There was a blue plaque over the door reading: *Anne Neville, Duchess of Gloucester, worked here, 1471.* Next to this hung a faded sign that said: *By appointment to His Grace the Duke of Clarence, purveyors of lark pasties and mutton pies.* A real class joint.

Roger sat me down in the corner, and ordered a gallon of draught claret and a swan pie. Apparently this was the Special.

"Bloody northerners!" grunted someone from the next embrasure. He had obviously taken exception to Roger's Gloucestershire accent, and probably to his White Boar livery badge as well. My husband put his hand to the hilt of his knife, and would have drawn it if I'd not trod on his foot under the table.

"Leave it out," I said, "Gloucester won't thank you if it kicks off in here. There are any number of Richard's retainers in London, and it's known that there are thousands of Yorkshiremen on their way as back-up. You can't expect the locals to like it. As far as they're concerned, we're only one step up from the Scots."

Roger muttered angrily, but he let it lie. "Had any luck?" he asked.

"Not really."

"Can't say I like what's going on," he added, "looking for excuses to deprive a boy of his inheritance. Not a great deal on that in the Knightly Code. Richard doesn't much like it either. He's in a grim mood. Grimmer than usual."

"It's what's called being on the horns of a dilemma, Husband."

He sighed. "At least we can have a rest tomorrow. Nothing much ever happens on a Sunday. Then on Monday young York's going to be fetched out of sanctuary. Richard wants both his nephews where he can see them."

The Duke of York, another Richard, was Elizabeth Woodville's younger son by King Edward. Unlike his brother, who had been brought up in his own household at Ludlow in the Marches, York had been kept close to her skirts.

"How exactly is that going to be arranged?" I asked. Sanctuary is, after all, sanctuary.

He shrugged. "By whatever means. The Cardinal Archbishop goes in first. If that doesn't work, there'll be eight boatloads of armed men to strengthen his arguments. Buckingham says that as York is only a boy, and hasn't committed any crime, he can't lay claim to sanctuary."

"I don't like the sound of that," I said. "It may be true, legally speaking, but it could produce a lot of bad publicity. Little boy being dragged away from his mummy by nasty northern soldiers. All that sort of thing. Not the image we want to build, is it?"

Roger shook his head. "The whole thing is going to throw up massive presentational problems. The business with Hastings hasn't helped. He had quite a fan club down here. Not just knights and squires, but merchants and even ordinary Joes. I don't think we've quite managed to persuade them all that he just suddenly decided to turn traitor."

"Richard was a shade hasty for his own good," I agreed. "To be honest, I think that Hastings was just playing politics. I don't believe he had anything to do with the poison, or even that he really wanted Richard toppled as Protector. He just didn't want things to tip too far one way. Unfortunately, he didn't realise that you don't mess with Richard like that without provoking an extremely negative response."

"There's also a lot of sympathy for Mistress Shore," Roger added.

Richard had arranged for Elizabeth Shore to do penance as a whore, which involved her walking through the streets of London in her shift, carrying a candle, and wearing a striped hood. (This did her no lasting harm. She ended up married to Thomas Lynom, the King's Solicitor, and lady of the manor of somewhere-or-other. You can't keep a good woman down, although in her case quite a few fellows had a damn good try.)

The pie had arrived, and we stopped our conversation for a few minutes while we dug into it. There's nothing like a nice hunk of swan when you're hungry, and after paying the London price for it we sure as hell didn't plan on leaving any for the dogs.

"There's a fellow I've not seen for a year or two," Roger said, pausing to spit a gobbet of gristle over the partition that divided us from the next table. (You can get away with that sort of thing if you're a knight and big with it.) He pointed uncertainly with his spoon. "Bishop of Bath and Wells. Shillingford or something. Used to hang around with George Clarence. Probably in town looking for a job. Edward kicked him out of the government years ago. Dare say he was a spot too close to George for comfort."

The Bishop did not look much like a bishop. More like a waste of space. He had about twenty-seven chins, and by the size of his belly had been living off the fat of the land all his life. After breaking off for a huge belch he picked up his pasty in his fingers, and munched away, blissfully unaware that it was dribbling gravy and sauce all over his shabby gown.

"Strikes me as a regular genius," I snorted.

"Appearances can be deceptive. You should know that, you empty-headed waiting-woman. He's a top man in his field. Canon Law and such stuff. Don't know how anyone can get interested in tedious tripe like that, but I suppose the answer is it pays well. You don't get a right lot of arrows shot at you, either. Not like my line of trade."

The claret was getting to me. I think I must have been sickening for something, as I'd only shifted about a pint. I let out a great yawn.

"I wonder how good he is on the validity of marriages?" I pondered. "We might have room on board for him after all. I'll check out his security file this afternoon, and then have a word with the head-hunters."

"You're going back to work? On Saturday afternoon?"

"With this rush job on I don't have much choice. Sorry, Roger, I gather you had something else in mind?"

"Dead right. And it wasn't sword practice, either."

I hated to disappoint him, but it was his own fault, after all, for getting me my job in the first place.

"After all this is sorted," I promised, "I'm going to resign. I don't mind staying on in Anne's service, if she wants me, but the intelligence side is going right out the door and no messing. I'm sick to the back teeth with all this independent career nonsense. I am going to be an ordinary knight's lady if it kills me."

The more I read about Bishop Stillington the more fascinated I became. He had four children by assorted mistresses and, more unusually for a bishop, had done time in the Tower after the fall of Clarence, and for no explicit reason. Here was another man who liked his juice, apt to say things under its influence that he later regretted. There were many references to scandalous remarks, touching the King's honour, although no specific quotations to justify the accusations.

But what was really interesting was that several pages had been torn from the file, none too carefully, leaving shreds of ripped parchment clinging to the binding. Security files are rarely weeded. Every irrelevant detail may one day become important, or at least useful. You rip out whole pages only when you want to hide inconvenient truth from your successors. It was an untidy, hasty piece of editing. I guessed that it had been done by someone senior, Hastings perhaps, or even the King himself, unconcerned by the prospect of detection. An Intelligence clerk would have made a much neater job of it.

I examined the torn stubs with care, but only the odd word survived. I was only able to find one that had any significance at all. The name, Eleanor.

There are plenty of women in England carrying that name, including some who spell it more attractively, but fortunately only a small minority of them justified a security file at Westminster. The cross-referencing system was up to the task, and after a couple of hours I turned up what I was looking for, another file that had been put on a reducing diet. In point of fact the file had been thinned out to the point where it might just as well have been thrown away. Its subject, Lady Eleanor Talbot, one of the daughters of the old Earl of Shrewsbury, had her marriage to Sir Thomas Butler recorded, her subsequent retiral to obscurity in Norfolk, where she took religious vows, and her death, but that was about all. Believe me, no one that ordinary ever has a file opened on them. It's too much hassle for the clerks.

It was then that I was hit by an inspiration. There were twenty-six files on Clarence, and I sent for the last of them. It had not been touched for years, and not a page was missing. There was report after report of George's drunken ravings, of his dealings with Stanley, and Oxford, and other dubious punters. And then there it was. A copy of a letter from George to Stillington, asking the Bishop to visit Warwick Castle, and to bring with him the proofs of the espousal of King Edward and Dame Eleanor Butler.

On its own I'd have put this down as one of George's delusions. But coupled with those edited files, and with the mystery that surrounded Clarence's death, it seemed to me that we had a runner.

"You really think that I should see this guy?" asked Richard, as he scanned through my written report.

"I do, Your Grace. Moreover, Francis agrees with me."

Lovel nodded. "It's certainly worth wheeling him in and asking a few questions. Even if the story doesn't stand up, we can be pretty sure that he isn't pro-Woodville. They had him stuck in the Tower for years. We could cope with an extra brace of reliable bishops about the place."

I could see even then that Gloucester was uncomfortable. Perhaps he didn't want to know the truth. Perhaps it just seemed to him that the truth was a shade too convenient to be really true.

"This letter from George doesn't prove a thing in itself," he objected. "In any event, it's only a copy, not an original. It could be a forgery."

"The Bishop will be able to give you the full show of betting," Lovel pointed out, "and, if Edward was pre-contracted to this Butler dame, then his children by Lizzie Woodville are bastards and you are the rightful King."

"There's George's boy," Richard reminded him.

"A half-wit! Only Lancastrians crown those! In any event, he's debarred by his father's attainder."

"All right, Francis. Let's give him the once over."

Stillington looked as worried as a flea in a lion's mouth. I think he had visions of spending several more years on Tower porridge.

Richard put on a very serious expression. The sort you select if you're about to declare war, or sentence someone to death.

"Right, Bishop," he said briskly. "I want to hear everything you know about Dame Eleanor Butler, down to her shoe size. And no lark-tongue pies, either, if you please."

(Richard was much sharper than people realised. He'd only been in London for a few weeks and he'd already picked up the local rhyming slang.)

The Bishop wrung his hands. I thought for a minute that he was going to cry. "But, Your Grace, I've been trying to get an appointment to see you for days. I don't know how you've come to hear of Eleanor Butler, because it was a close secret, but it's all horribly true. I saw them married. Truly it was so."

"You saw Eleanor Butler married to Sir Thomas Butler? Is that the big secret?"

The Bishop shook his chins. "I witnessed her marriage to your brother, King Edward. Long before he'd even heard of Elizabeth Woodville. That's the point I'm trying to make."

Richard seemed to slump in his chair, and he rested his head in his hands. You'd have thought that he'd just lost everything, not gained it.

"So it's true," he said, very quietly. "Now I understand why it was that my brother, Clarence, had to die. He had learned of this."

"Yes, Your Grace. And he was all too apt to talk of it while under the influence of alcoholic beverages. Of course, Eleanor Butler died some years ago, but that does not make King Edward's children legitimate, even those born after her demise."

He went on to explain why this was, but it was all very complex and boring, to do with the doctrines of Canon Law, and I've long since forgotten the full details. In fact I forgot them before I heard them. It was, however, quite clear that Richard was our lawful King. We had, as they say in archery circles, struck gold.

The big mistake was to put the publicity job into Buckingham's hands. He made a complete hash of it, engaging some chap called Dr Ralph Shaa to preach on the subject at Paul's Cross the Sunday following. Either Shaa was given an inadequate brief or he didn't bother to read it. Instead of sticking to the simple story of Eleanor Talbot-Butler, he rambled on for hours about the dubious legitimacy of King Edward IV, the silly fable that we had dumped back at first base. This was a disgraceful insult to Richard's mother, and didn't exactly show Richard himself up in a good light, since everyone naturally assumed that he had authorised the script. Half the folk had gone home by the time Shaa got around to telling them the bit that he should have told them in the first place, and it probably didn't sink in with the other half, who were now more interested in their dinner than in matters of politics.

Buckingham then gathered the chief citizens together, and made a speech that was so lousy and inept that the Mayor – who was Ralph Shaa's brother, by the way – had to get the City Recorder to repeat it to the punters in language that they could understand. The whole sales pitch went down like a goblet of chilled vomit, a total public relations disaster.

I'm convinced that this was all deliberate sabotage. However, if you prefer to believe that Buckingham was grossly incompetent, incapable of arranging for an excessive intake of alcohol at a church-ale, then I shall not gainsay you.

Anyway, to cut a long story short, the assembled evidence was passed around the available lords, bishops, and other opinion-formers, and a petition was drawn up asking Richard to accept the Crown. Richard said he would, if they insisted, and we all adjourned to make ready for the Coronation.

The next few days went by in something of a blur. The entire household was up to its collective neck in the preparations, and I seemed to spend most of my time helping Anne with the fitting sessions for her gowns. Intelligence work just had to go on hold, and I was not even able to follow up on an interesting report that an Italian cleric called Mancini was busily despatching distorted tales of our doings to our enemies in France. This fellow could not even speak English, so he must have really struggled to get hold of anything useful. French Intelligence are a clueless lot at the best of times, but I expect that even they were able to figure out that his stuff wasn't worth the parchment it was written on.

Anne had lost weight. (The Queen, that is. I always did have to keep reminding myself.) I couldn't decide whether it was down to the worry, or whether she was ill. She'd slimmed to such an extent that she could get into one of the new, low-waisted gowns without lacing herself up in a corset. (By the way, if I ever find the bastard who decided that the fashion needed changing, I promise that I shall find half the cost of having him buried cheaply. Things have gone steadily downhill since the first time that I had my breath squeezed out of me by tight lacing, and I suspect that the whole thing is nothing but a Tudor conspiracy against the women of England.)

Talking of the Tudor, I find it is now often forgotten that that nasty little man's mother, Margaret Beaufort, carried Anne's train on Coronation Day. This was undoubtedly a sop to her husband, Sneaky Stanley, and I cite it as further proof that he was not involved in the Hastings conspiracy. He himself could be found walking about with the Lord High Constable's mace of office clutched in his sweaty paw, grinning like one who'd just found a gold coin in the middle of a pickled onion.

It was a great day of celebration, although a wearying one in the July heat. We had a banquet at which we stuffed ourselves for hours, and we concluded proceedings by setting off a large box of fireworks.

The only thing that worried me was the expression that crossed Buckingham's face as Richard was crowned. He could scarcely bring himself to watch. It wasn't as if Richard had not been generous to him. He'd been too damned generous by half in my opinion, giving him virtual control of Wales for a start. But the likes of Buckingham are never satisfied. If you offer them a guarantee of admission to Heaven, they ask for the office of sword bearer to God and the hand of a female saint in marriage. You have to keep an eye on men like that.

IX

Those of you who enjoy analysing petty details will have noted that this Chronicle is written in several different styles of handwriting. This is because I have frequently used an amanuensis. Lest future generations be misled, I wish to record that I, Alianore Audley, alias Dame Alianore Beauchamp, am well able to form my letters for myself when so inclined. However, to avoid an aching wrist, I prefer to dictate to some other person when possible. Many of these pages, and almost all of those that contain foul language, have been inscribed by my faithful chaplain, Sir Walter Gloy, who has stuck to me through thick and thin.

Another gentleman who assisted me for a time, during a brief visit to Horton Beauchamp, was Bishop Russell, formerly Chancellor to King Richard. I was amazed at the speed of the good Bishop's pen, and do believe that if we had both had sufficient leisure he could easily have got the whole thing down within ten days.

Other sections have been written by Francis, Viscount Lovel, as a method of passing time during his occasional sojourns with us. Francis also helped by correcting my understanding of certain events, but as I have not seen him now for some years I begin to fear that he has come to harm. Or perhaps he's just living quietly in a secret room somewhere. Who knows? At least he has not fallen into the hands of that splendid fellow, Mr Tudor. We should certainly have heard all about it if he had.

It was to Francis that I handed over my responsibilities for Yorkist Intelligence. I put my papers in immediately after the

Coronation, carefully explaining that I was not resigning over any matter of policy, but because I wanted to spend more time with my family. Richard gave me a funny look, but when I added that I was only too happy to stay on in Anne's service he relaxed a little.

"Don't fly off to Gloucestershire just yet," he ordered. "I've a little job in mind for you and Roger. May be a month or two before I've got things in place, and then I'll tell you all about it."

I didn't like the sound of that, but I knew that there was no point in making waves. If your King gives you work you do not refuse it. It says so in the Knightly Code.

The next day I received a fresh Commission, with Richard's signature still wet on the parchment, and I began to doubt whether I should ever be allowed to call it a day. It was my own fault for making myself so useful. I always knew I should have stuck to the embroidery.

After a little time at Greenwich, the Court set out on a Progress. A Progress is always a sign of weakness, as no king who feels truly secure on his throne ever bothers to show himself to his subjects north of St Alban's or west of Reading, but we needed the publicity. Unfortunately, the Queen travelled no further than Windsor before the heat got to her and she had to let Richard travel on without her. When I learned that his itinerary included several days at Oxford listening to boring old academics rattling on about obscure points of philosophy, I was more than content to keep Anne company.

It was not long before word came to us of a thwarted plot to bust the two Princes out of the Tower. The people involved included some minor members of Richard's own household, which was not good for morale.

"I hope this isn't going to happen every week," said Anne. You would have thought, from her tone of voice, that it was all my fault.

"You can expect every malcontent in England to make use of the boys," I replied. "Just as they once made use of old Harry the Sixth. It's in the way of nature. If you don't like your king you cast around to see what else is available."

"That's why deposed kings are usually murdered," Anne observed.

"Yes," I agreed, remembering Mad Harry, who, it must be said, had been quite harmless in himself and yet still a potent threat to King Edward. "Yes, that's quite true. But we're dealing with young boys here, and taking them out would very bad for Richard's image. Disastrous, in fact. Even then, you'd still be left with the five girls: Elizabeth, Cecily, Katherine, Anne, and Bridget. How could he possibly slaughter all of them? Next, to be really safe, he'd have to do something with George's son and daughter. And after that, he'd still have to pop over to Brittany to sort out Henry Tudor."

"Who the hell is Henry Tudor?" Anne asked, her brow furrowing.

"Margaret Beaufort's son. He reckons to be the Lancastrian heir, although his claim is so incredibly feeble and obscure that only a madman or a loving mother would advance it. The point is that there's always someone else. You can't kill them all. It's better to rely on the fact that young Edward and his brother are bastards. People will get used to that idea after a while, especially when they discover that they've copped for a pretty decent sort of king in Richard."

"I hope you're right," she sighed.

"You bet your sceptre I am," I said.

By the time we rejoined Richard, up at Warwick, there had been a considerable improvement in the smell of the Court. Buckingham had gone home to Brecon. He had Morton in prison there, and I guessed that he was planning on a quiet month of torturing or something. How wrong can one woman be?

We moved on to York, where Richard and Anne's son, brought down from Middleham for the occasion, was invested as Prince of Wales. It was another lavish ceremony, but the public relations value was tremendous, and the people of York gave us the kind of reception that Tudor, the Walking Emetic, will never find anywhere but in his dreams.

Of course, there always has to be something to spoil even the best of days. Roger and I were called out of bed at midnight to attend an urgent conference. Lovel had received a lengthy despatch from our top agent in London, concerning the wild rumours that were flying around. Half the population of southern England already believed that the Princes were murdered, while the other half were involved in various plots to release them. The Woodvilles had been stirring it good and proper in our absence, and there was a hint, though no more, that they had someone else pulling strings on their behalf.

By the same post there was a letter to Richard himself from Brackenbury, the Lieutenant of the Tower. Someone had had a shot at poisoning the Princes.

"Not strawberries again?" asked Roger.

Richard shook his head. "Give them some credit for imagination. Sweetmeats. Delivered by a man in my livery."

"We can't pin this on the Woodvilles," I said. "They'd be the last to want to harm the boys. So that means we're getting hassle from another quarter."

"I'd figured that out for myself," the King grunted. "The question is, what to do about it."

"Difficult," murmured James Tyrell. He was a dark-haired and rather wiry knight, Richard's Master of Horse, one of those chaps who are taciturn but utterly reliable.

"I've already set an investigation in train," announced Lovel. "The suspects are pretty obvious, really. Henry Tudor, in Brittany, and his saintly mother, Margaret Beaufort, Lady Stanley. The

Countess of Richmond as she likes to call herself. They have most to gain."

"How?" asked Anne, yawning. She had not troubled to get out of bed. She had just wrapped her chamber-robe about her.

"Kill the boys and you make Elizabeth, their eldest sister, King Edward's heir. If you discount their bastardy, that is. If he married her, Tudor would do much to strengthen his pathetic claim."

"Then why not announce that Tudor has tried to murder the lads?" suggested Roger. "It'd be good propaganda, even if it turns out not to be strictly true."

Richard shook his head. "I feel inclined to keep a low profile. Say it turns out that one of my friends has done this, trying to please me? If that's how it lies no one will ever believe that I wasn't involved. Besides, why give Tudor the oxygen of publicity? An unknown Welshman, whose father I never knew, nor him personally saw! His name is scarcely known outside intelligence circles. Least said, soonest mended. The boys had better disappear for a while. I've had it in mind, and it looks like it better not be left any longer. You, with Alianore, and Tyrell here, will take them to my sister in Burgundy, and they can stay there until things cool down. All to be done in secrecy, of course. You will also arrange for a strengthening of the security cordon around Westminster Sanctuary. I don't want any of Edward's daughters going missing and turning up in Brittany. Any questions?"

I reckon that we set a new record for the trip to London. King Edward – or rather Hastings – had organised a chain of exchange points for horses all along the Great North Road so that government messengers could make good time. We cut sleeping, eating, and the other natural functions of life down to a bare minimum, picked up fresh mounts at every opportunity, and made it to the capital in less than three days.

We went straight to the Tower, pausing only to despatch a boy round to Westminster with a note to tell John Nesfield, who was in charge there, to quadruple the guard around the Sanctuary.

I found a cushion to sit on while the men talked things through with Brackenbury. I needed it after that journey, believe me.

"I've put t' boys in closer ward since," Brackenbury told us. He was an oldish fellow, bald as a shaven egg, and very worried. A decent sort, but none too sure of himself when dealing with the heavy stuff. "The elder of 'em, young Ned, gone to pieces, he has. Expects to die at any minute. Spends all his time praying. Doesn't help that I can't let 'em out into t' garden any more. Used to like a bit of shooting with bows and that. And it got a bit o' fresh air into t' lads. But I reckoned it were too public by half for 'em, after t' warnings we've had. Don't know who's poking and prying. Caught a fellow called Dighton sneaking round with a pillow t' other night. Reckoned as how he was off looking for his young woman, but I weren't for teking chances, not after what's gone down 'ere up to now. Sent him on his way pretty sharpish."

"It's a damned bad show when they're not safe in the Tower, of all places," grunted Tyrell.

"They are safe, for now," objected Brackenbury. "But just you think back to when you were a lad. What sort of life is it for 'em, to be kept in a maximum security lodging, with bars over t'' windows and no chance to see as much as a blade o' grass?"

"Sooner we get them to Burgundy the better," Roger said briskly. "It's the getting them there in secrecy that's the problem. I don't know how it's to be done. They're well known in London, especially the younger boy, and there must be umpteen spies around, watching for any sign of them being moved. Any security leak could be a disaster."

"We could lay a few false trails," suggested Tyrell. "Mention Sheriff Hutton in an alehouse or two. Murmur about Ireland somewhere else. We could say that they tried to escape, and that one of them fell in the Thames and drowned. We could even get hold of a big box, fill it with stones, and bury it under one of the Tower staircases. A good deep hole that takes a long time to dig and as long to fill in again. Preferably somewhere where there's plenty of traffic to be interrupted so that people talk about it."

"The first three sound good. I don't think anyone would be taken in by the other. It's too obvious. But even after laying the false trails, we're still landed with the job of getting them out of here undetected. Any ideas anyone?"

"They could travel as my waiting-women," I said.

"As what?" cried Roger.

"In our haste from York we left ourselves somewhat lightly attended to be ambassadors to the Duchess of Burgundy. Bear in mind that we shall be rolling up at one of the most formal Courts in Europe. You've got Arthur, and Sir James has got his man, but I'm rather conspicuously free of anyone to wait on me. The lads could fill in. It'd be an interesting experience for them."

"I suspect they'd sooner die."

"You could," I said, "give them the option."

It was a long time since I had set eyes on either one of Elizabeth Woodville's boys, and I had quite forgotten how handsome they were. All princes are handsome, of course, but these two remained so as bastards, and would still have shone as bricklayers.

It was a pity that the elder, Ned, was something of a weed. As soon as the door opened he started to whimper and we found him clutching his brother as if young Dickon was a rag doll.

"The m... murderers are here," he stammered.

"Sir," I said, forcibly, "these gentlemen are knights. Knights do not murder boys. They get contractors in to do such jobs for them. Moreover, it would be entirely against Court etiquette for them to murder even a grown man in my presence. You are quite safe."

That calmed them down a little, and we were able to introduce ourselves.

"Uncle Richard has already had one crack at us," said Dickon fiercely. "Now he's shut us up in here, and taken all our old servants from us. I'm bored rigid. Why doesn't he get it over with? He's already killed our Uncle Rivers, and our half-brother, Richard Grey. What is he waiting for?"

"Rivers and Grey were guilty of high treason, as you are not," Roger explained, with admirable patience I thought. "You are confined here for security reasons, and for your own safety."

"So he can poison us more easily," Ned whimpered.

"The King had no hand in that. It's likely that it was the work of rebel elements favourable to Henry Tudor."

"Henry Tudor?"

"An obscure cousin of yours, who seeks to discredit the King for his own purposes."

"Aye," grunted Tyrell, "and how better to do that than by branding him a murderer of children? After all, no one can deny that King Richard is responsible for your safety. Bastards you may be, but you are still in his care. The trouble is that, even so close confined as you are, there's no guarantee that these scum will not find a way to get at you."

"That's why it's necessary for you to disappear from men's sight," Roger went on. "In Burgundy the Duchess your aunt should be able to arrange for you to live a more normal life. No one there, apart from her, will know you from Adam. Tell them the plan, Alianore."

It was like Roger to leave the easy bit to me. The boys, I have to say, were not mad keen on the idea. I think what swung it in the end was their realisation that it was the only way that they were going to get out of the Tower. With so many enemy agents about, we couldn't run the risk of anyone tracing them to Burgundy.

"It is only until we get to Aunt Margaret's, isn't it?" asked Dickon.

"Of course it is. I can assure that it will be no worse for you than it was for me when I had to dress up as one of Warwick's archers. As you can see, there are no long-term effects."

"You were an archer, my lady?" Ned asked, gaping.

"Yes, I was. I sure as hell didn't enjoy it at the time, but it gave me a new window on life. Just look on this as a learning opportunity."

"All right then," he said, sulkily. "Anything to get out of this dump. Just don't expect us to like it."

"I'd be more worried if you did," I said.

As luck would have it, Brackenbury had two daughters of about the right sizes, and we were able to send them around the fripperers of London to obtain suitable second-hand clothing. Roger and James Tyrell began to spread a few crazy rumours around, often getting drunk in the process so as to make it more convincing, while Brackenbury arranged for some highly suspicious excavations at the Tower, under the direction of a trusted priest. A couple of skeletons were found at the bottom of the hole, which threw us into some confusion. However, as Brackenbury pointed out to us, the Tower has been an inhabited site since Roman times. (Julius Caesar allegedly issued the first building contract.) Over the years, many people have been buried and forgotten. We put an old velvet cloak over the bones, had the priest say a mass for them, and covered them up again.

While all this was going on I had the task of coaching the boys for their new roles. This, perforce, had to be something of a crash course, enabling them to walk without tripping over their gowns, to turn without tangling their legs in their skirts, and to curtsey without falling over.

"Listen," I said, after they had more or less mastered these basics, "I can't possibly teach you all the tricks of being a damosel in so short a time. These are the guidelines. Keep your mouth closed. Walk slowly, with small steps, and try not to flash too much hose-cloth, especially when you're dealing with stairs or climbing on a horse. Keep your eyes downcast. When you sit down, keep your ankles crossed. Blush as much as possible. And if any man tries anything on, just imagine that he's got a football between his legs, and try to score a goal with it. From thirty yards."

Roger arrived just at that moment. You could see that he was doing his best not to laugh.

"How is it going?" he asked.

"I don't think that they'd stand close inspection," I sighed, "but with any luck they shouldn't have to. It's not as if we're seeking marriages for them, is it?"

"Their bridegrooms would certainly find a few things lacking!" Roger chortled. He was enjoying himself, even if no one else was.

"I could name some men who'd think their boat had come in," I muttered, "but that's beside the point. Have you made all the travel arrangements?"

He nodded. "A King's ship from Dover. Captained by Sir Edward Brampton."

"We know him!" squealed Dickon enthusiastically. "Our father's godson."

"And, of course," Roger went on, "a litter from here to Dover for you and the girls."

"Don't push it, Sir Roger," snapped Ned.

"It's as well to think of yourselves in those terms until we get to Flanders," I said. "Remember, you're acting a part. Slip out of character for a couple of minutes and you'll give the whole game away, and perhaps put your lives at risk. Once you're safe with your aunt you can stomp and swear and pick your noses to your hearts' content, but for the present you're Edwina and Richildis, and you'll bear yourself accordingly."

"Yes, my lady," simpered Dickon. He made quite a decent tilt at a curtsey, but took things just that bit too far, and fell on his behind. He found this most amusing. I bit my tongue, remembering the days when I'd have got a week on bread and water for a mistake like that. At least he was getting into the spirit of things.

We left London by way of the Bridge, and as it was first thing in the morning we ran into all the incoming traffic from Southwark and the southern suburbs. I don't know what fool decided to make the Bridge so narrow, but it's awkward for litters at the best of times, unless you've got a company of archers to hold back the plebs, and we were stuck in the crush for the best part of an hour. I suppose that one day someone will get around to constructing a second bridge, but God knows when that will be. It's only been needed for about two hundred years, after all.

The boys would keep leaning out to see what was going on, and I lived in constant fear of someone recognising them. People were having a much closer look at us than was comfortable, and I wasn't sure that we were going to pass muster. I fondled the butt of the hand-gonne I had bought in preparation for the hazards of the journey, then remembered that it was quite useless unless I could find a way to light the slow-match that went with it.

"Edwina, sit still!" I snapped. "Richildis, remember that you are supposed to be a young gentlewoman, and stop goggling at everyone! Put your backs straight and be quiet, both of you."

"That's right, my lady," said a plump dame, leaning in over the very door of the litter. "These youngsters nowadays! No respect for their elders at all. Don't know where the world's coming to, I don't. It's not like it used to be when we were young, in good King Harry's time. Give them a damn good thrashing, that's my counsel. Never did us any harm, did it?"

"Madam," I answered, rude in my haste to be rid of her, "I am not likely to take advice about the ordering of my household from a woman in a dirty coverchief, and most certainly not in the middle of the public highway. Be so good as to sod off."

She scowled and pushed back into the crowd. "Stuck-up cow," she complained to her friend. "Get a four horse litter and a bit of a place at Court and they think they own the Bridge. All the same, these northerners. Not used to having money, that's their trouble."

Roger had also been caught up in conversation, with a knight, Sir George Browne, he knew from his days in King Edward's service.

"Didn't know you had any lands south of the Thames, Beauchamp," Sir George bellowed.

"Nor do I," said Roger. "We're just off to Canterbury for St Thomas's shrine. The wife hasn't seen it yet. Have you, my dear?"

I inclined my head, and tried not to smile as Browne's horse backed up and stood on a man's foot. The fellow dropped his basket of oysters and ran through the complete London catalogue of abusive terms. The boys sniggered helplessly.

"Tyrell here is going along for the ride," Roger continued, "and to look for a suitable wife for his son."

"Dead right," nodded Sir James, "and I'm also in the market for any decent horses that are going. That's not a bad one you're sitting on, Browne. Fancy selling him to the King?"

Sir George ignored this question, as well as the curses rising from the gutter. "I hear from my nephew, Paston, that there are some very strange rumours afloat about the young Princes," he ventured. "Even that they're dead. You two are much closer to the King than I am. When can we expect an official statement from the government?"

"No comment," said Tyrell.

"You shouldn't believe everything you hear in the alehouses," Roger added. "The King will make an announcement in his own good time, but I wouldn't advise you to press him for it."

"Ah, well," sighed Browne, "just don't be surprised if you come across a fair amount of grutching and grumbling as you travel through Kent. Even the odd fool tattling about some conspiracy or other. All hot air, of course. It won't come to anything. We're all staunchly loyal. But people will talk. Especially the lower orders, you know. They get such wild ideas in their heads."

It always arouses my suspicions when a man makes a point of stressing his own loyalty, and some inner voice told me that Browne's security file needed a thorough checking. However, it was only a hunch, and I was in no position to do anything about it. I had enough on my plate keeping the two boys in order.

X

The writing of this Chronicle has been interrupted by the arrival of our neighbour, Sir Humphrey Berkeley, who has told me that he wishes to marry my daughter. One cannot afford to be too choosy these days, and so he may have to do for her, even if he did fight for Tudor at Bosworth.

Constance herself seems less than impressed with him. She appears to think him disqualified as a potential husband by his advanced age – he is past fifty – his huge belly and his sour breath. I don't know where the girl has got such romantic notions. Certainly not from me. Perhaps from her father. Roger was born into the wrong century. He'd have been much happier back with William Marshal, or Roland, or some other armour-polisher. He could have gone around slaying dragons, and rescuing damosels from towers.

I hope I don't have to persuade her to do her duty. I find nowadays that I can't give anyone a really good beating without my arm aching for a week afterwards. I must be getting past it.

As I told her, the advantage of marrying an old man is that he is likely to be worn out in no time. Before you know it, he's dead, and you're left with nothing but a fat jointure to comfort you. Once you have security of tenure you can afford a little romance, if you're that way inclined.

Guy has also been to see me, to inform me that we have some surplus malt that needs to be sold off before it rots. I don't know what he expects me to do about it. Ride into Gloucester, perhaps, and hire a stall in the market. I find these days that there's always someone pestering me over some trifling matter. Roger has written from London, bidding me go to the Sheriff and obtain a writ of Replevin, whatever that may be, against our neighbour, Berkeley. Something to do with our cattle finding their way onto his land and not coming back. First I've heard of it, and how Roger has learned of it is beyond me. I tell you, I had a quieter life when I was working for Yorkist Intelligence, and it was a damn sight more interesting. I think I shall write to ask Roger what I'm to do with the malt. It'll give the impression that I don't do anything without his instructions, which should please him no end. I do hope he remembers to bring my new girdle home with him. And the scarlet gown I hinted about in my last letter. Of course, I shan't be at all sarcastic if he lets me down.

Guy, by the way, has become our Steward at Horton Beauchamp. He's a grizzled fellow now, and his eyesight is not quite what it was, so he's retired from competitive archery and taken on a desk job. He settled down, not long after Tewkesbury, with a nice young shepherdess he found somewhere towards Burford and they've produced quite a quiver of little arrows over the subsequent years.

I owe a lot to Guy. After all, he did save my life. And he led me to the church door, when not even one of my own brothers could be bothered to put in an appearance. As far as I'm concerned he's part of the family, and always will be. It's a pity he hasn't got a coat of arms, especially in these days when any little rat can buy one from Mr Tudor if he's got the wit to forge a pedigree for himself. I can think of a pushy family from Northampton way who've done exactly that. They claim to be descended from the Despensers of all people. Well, my grandmother was wife to a Despenser before she met my grandfather, and I can assure you that those damned graziers are no relations at all. Cheeky rogues! I absolutely refuse to be connected to them. They're the kind that clear their tenants from the land to accommodate more sheep, and bring the whole ruling class into disrepute. Dwelling on their success only confirms me in my opinion that England is finished.

It was not easy to get in to see the Lady Margaret of York, Duchess of Burgundy. Her Court at Malines was very formal, and you had to study a manual of etiquette and hand over a copy of your pedigree before they would even let you through the door. A solemn lady, Duchess Margaret, very much like her brother, King Richard, both in looks and demeanour. A woman born to wear black if I have ever met one.

We were kept in her waiting-room for quite a long time. Behind a grille was her collection of books and manuscripts, which was almost as big as Margaret Beaufort's. There was a portrait of her late husband, Duke Charles, and, next to it, a series of illustrations of Margaret herself doing good works – visiting prisoners, attending funerals, handing out alms, and so on. Her image consultant had obviously told her that piety was a strong selling point in Flanders.

She did not even snicker when she saw her nephews in their highly inappropriate attire. Instead she gave them each a brief hug and told one of her women to take them into her private apartments. Before they went, the two boys very politely thanked us for our trouble.

"Come on," cried Dickon at last, "let's get out of these things and find a ball to kick around. I've forgotten what my legs look like."

"I hope you can manage without us, Dame Beauchamp," said Ned, grinning. "I never realised how difficult it was to get in and out of a woman's gown."

Margaret frowned, and waited until they were gone. Then she seated herself, on a big chair that stood under a cloth-of-estate.

"The King my brother should have had more sense than to send them here," she said, her eyes fixed somewhere above our heads. "We have our own political difficulties, as he should be well aware. We are overrun with French agents, and those fellows are undoubtedly swapping notes with Henry Tudor, or whatever his name is."

"Is Madame implying that the Lords Bastard will not be safe here?" Tyrell asked.

"Madame is more than implying it," snapped Margaret. "Tell Richard that he had better come up with a more secure hiding place for them and pretty damned quick."

We stared at each other uncomfortably. We'd never thought for a minute that they'd be in any danger in Margaret's domains.

"Perhaps, Madame, if the boys were to live here under assumed names," Roger suggested. "One in one household, one in another. There is nothing, after all, to connect them with your nephews."

She snorted. "Of course not! Flanders is full of boys who speak only English and look like Plantagenets! Tell my brother that he must make other arrangements as soon as possible."

There was no point in arguing with her. She was like Richard in that as well. We made our way out of the room, counting off our obeisances as we backed away and hoping that we'd understood the instructions in the manual. It doesn't do to be thought ill-mannered.

Roger and I returned to Horton Beauchamp, while Tyrell rode off north to report to the King. I was looking forward to my new life of retirement, and I rolled up my sleeves and got down to the October brewing. All the children helped with this, while my husband devoted himself to reducing the number of deer in our park.

Then it began to rain. And rain. And rain.

Later, men called it the Duke of Buckingham's Water. Well, if it was, all I can say is that he must have had a hell of a lot to drink.

Roger and I gave up and retired to bed. Hunting isn't much fun in torrential rain, and making ale is nowhere near as enjoyable as making the beast with two backs.

Afternoon or no, it was pitch black in our chamber, and we didn't even bother to draw the curtains around the bed. I submitted twice to my husband's lust, gritting my teeth as one does on such occasions. I was just in the middle of arranging matters so that I would have to submit to it once more when we were interrupted by a discreet cough. It was Guy. Again.

"Guy," I said angrily, "this is the second time in twelve years. You'd better have a bloody good excuse."

"Sorry, my lady. A letter from the King, marked *urgent* and some chap in livery waiting downstairs for an answer."

Roger tore the letter open. I could see from his face that we had big trouble. "Buckingham is revolting," he cried, already half out of bed.

"I know that," I said.

"I mean he's up in arms. Against the King."

I had to read it for myself before I could believe it. Buckingham, beguiled by that rat Morton, had turned against Richard. He was raising men in Wales, proclaiming his support for Henry Tudor, and half the gentlemen of southern England, from Kent round to Dorset, had risen with him. The Woodvilles were part of it, of course, but there were others with them, including Sir George Browne. Morton was busily spreading rumours that King Edward's sons were murdered. And Tudor, having sworn to marry their eldest sister Elizabeth of York, was on his way with an army to invade us.

"Margaret Beaufort is behind this," I snarled. "She pulls Morton's strings to serve that poxy son of hers."

Roger was appointed a Commissioner of Array for Gloucestershire, which made it his business to set about raising men for the King, rain or no rain. He wasted no time. There were two or three days of hustle and bustle, with urgent messages going off in all directions pleading for more recruits, and then he was off to meet Lovel at Banbury, stripping the manor of almost every man under sixty. He left Guy behind to protect me, much to Guy's disgust. Horton Beauchamp was suddenly a very quiet place.

"Fancy a trip behind enemy lines?" I asked.

"Sir Roger won't like it," Guy predicted gloomily.

"I'm not proposing anything too dangerous," I explained. "Just a little visit to my kinsmen, the Vaughans of Tretower. In Wales."

"I didn't know you had any kinsmen in Wales, my lady."

"I've kin all over the place. My sister Margaret married into that lot, before she went on to be wedded to Lord Grey of Powys. The Vaughans are a big family. There's umpteen branches of them, and I never did manage to work out their full pedigree. Anyway, I dare say they're all my cousins by courtesy. Even if they're not, I'll swear to God that they are. The point is that they're good Yorkists, support King Richard and hate the very sight of Buckingham, so we should be able to stir a few pots with them."

A toothy grin spread over Guy's face. Within an hour, we were on the road.

It was quite a journey. The rain was endless, and I was soaked all the way through to my skin and out again before we got so far as Gloucester. The roads were one big quagmire, and we found bridges broken down and fords impassable, so there were any number of diversions. I don't know how we ever got to Tretower without swimming, but we did.

The Vaughans were holding a Council of War when we arrived, but they welcomed us and sat us down with a large bowl of broth each and about half a dozen blankets. The Welsh are a very hospitable people, especially when you can claim kindred.

There seemed to be any number of Vaughans present in the hall, a formidable bunch, dark-browed and muscular, and obviously very wound up. Some of them spoke in English, some in Welsh, and some in a mixture of the two, and they seemed to be holding a competition to see who could describe Buckingham in the most abusive terms. (They didn't go much for Tudor, either. This may surprise those of you who are under the absurd delusion that the entire Welsh nation thinks that the sun goes out whenever he sits down, but the Vaughans had some kind of hereditary feud with his Uncle Jasper.) They weren't going to need much urging from me, that was clear.

"May I make a little suggestion?" I asked.

Thomas Vaughan, the head of the family, made a gracious gesture towards me. I think he expected me to point out that the broth needed a tad more in the way of salt, or that one of the wall-hangings needed a stitch or two to stop it fraying.

"Buckingham has left his castle at Brecon behind him. It isn't very far from here, is it? I should think that he'd be jolly cross if someone went along and set fire to it. Of course, one could remove a few things first. I dare say that there's the odd valuable lying around."

I could tell that I'd hit the right note. A faraway gleam came into their eyes, and some of them started banging their weapons on the table. (A disgusting habit this, and one that I would never allow in my household.) At the far end of the hall a chap started plucking at a harp, and before I knew what was happening the whole room had burst into song. The words were in Welsh, and so I haven't the vaguest clue what it was all about, but it sure as hell wasn't a lullaby.

The Vaughans were quite amused when they discovered that I was planning to go with them to Brecon, but they didn't give me any serious hassle. We set off first thing in the morning, before it was properly light, and I rode next to Thomas Vaughan himself, at the head of the procession. I was amazed by just how many men were following us. I've no idea where they all came from at such short notice, unless there's a trapdoor leading to an underground kingdom in that part of the world, but I'd be very surprised if there were less than a thousand in the tail. Each time we came to a clump of trees, or some fork in the road, a few more rolled up to join in the fun.

Thomas Vaughan handed me a strip of red cloth, and told me to tie it about my right arm. He gave another piece to Guy.

"What are these for?" I asked.

"Field signs. Any man not wearing one is likely to end up dead, see."

"Surely a woman will not be harmed, will she?"

He grinned, showing off his huge teeth. "Not killed, perhaps. But some of my boys are, as you might say, apt to get a little carried away on these occasions. Better to be safe than sorry."

"I was rather hoping we could keep the lid on civilian casualties. King Richard already has serious image problems, you know."

"Oh, we'll keep it to a minimum, right enough," said Vaughan airily. He turned to one of his brothers, and muttered something in Welsh that set them both laughing.

I delved into the folds of my gown, and drew out my Commission. I opened it, and handed it to Vaughan. It said:

To whom it may concern:

The bearer of these presents, Dame Alianore Beauchamp, enjoys our full confidence and is acting in accordance with our commands.

All Sheriffs, Mayors, Constables, Bailiffs, and others of our Officers are ordered to render her their full assistance.

RICARDUS REX

P.S.

Anyone not complying with this Instruction will receive Extremely Negative Vibrations. RR

(This last bit was written in Richard's own hand, at my request.)

This took some of the wind out of Vaughan's sails. You could see he was impressed.

"All right," he conceded. "We'll just kill those who resist. That's fair enough, is it?"

I nodded. "I've no problem with that. And, of course, there's nothing to stop you looting the castle from top to bottom. I'm sure the King will be only too pleased to give you a grant of everything you liberate. Though I'd not bother with Buckingham's wardrobe if I were you. Violet won't go with your eyes."

He laughed. "We'll burn what we don't take. It should be quite a day out, one way and another."

The garrison of Brecon were not expecting an attack. The gates were open, the drawbridge was down, and people were wandering in and out as they fancied. I'd expected to have to come up with some brilliant plan to get us in, and I was deeply disappointed to find that I'd been cudgelling my brains for nothing.

There was an odd arrow shot at us, and a few half-hearted blows struck, but the defenders were a handful of boys and old men, and they had the sense not to make too many objections. The Vaughans flooded everywhere, breaking down doors and smashing windows in their haste to get to the portable property, and I dived into my saddlebag, searching for my hand-gonne. I primed it carefully, and got a light for my slow-match from the torch carried by a passing Vaughan on his way to fire the granary.

"Useless things those," grunted Guy. "You mark my words."

"They're a bit handier than a longbow when you're working indoors," I answered. "Plus you don't need strength to fire one. Don't be so damned old-fashioned. Come with me. We're looking for Buckingham's papers, especially letters from the other conspirators. It's vital evidence, and the Vaughans are likely to burn it if we don't get to it first. Leave everything else to our friends."

"A few gold coins would come in handy," he objected.

"You'll get more than a few, and from the King himself, if we pull this off. Come on."

It was chaos in the castle, as you can imagine, with women screaming, children bawling, dogs barking and the Vaughans smashing their way into everything, tearing down tapestries, and knocking Buckingham's furniture all over the shop.

We had to start somewhere. I decided to slip through a doorway at the dais end of the hall, and climb the stairs into the upper chambers. Guy was right behind me, his bow slung over his shoulder and a damned big knife, an anelace, in his hand. There were Vaughans ahead of us, arguing about the revised ownership arrangements for the chapel furnishings. We went further up the stairs, and came to a parting of the ways.

"Try in there," I told Guy. "I'll go up to the next floor."

The stairs beyond this point were a lot narrower, and damp from the rain that had poured in through an arrow slit. I really needed three hands at this point, one for my gonne, one for my slow-match, and one for my skirts, and however I arranged matters the two provided by God were not really able to cope with the task. I slipped and caressed the stonework with my forehead.

"Oh, dear!" I said. "How frightfully irritating!"

When I reached the top of the stairs I emerged into what was a large and surprisingly well-lit room. It was so bright that I was able to see that when I'd fallen I'd managed to burn a hole in my gown with the slow-match.

"Oh, dear!" I said again. Or at least, I said something along those general lines.

I reverted to my inspection of the room. It contained six clerks' desks, on each of which was a portion of a newly written Chronicle. There were umpteen copies in all, purporting to be a history of the reign of King Richard III, and containing the most unimaginable lies. Richard was supposed to have sent men to the Tower to smother the Princes with pillows, but that was only the start of it. He had stabbed Henry VI to death with his own hand, drowned Clarence, and slain a helpless Prince Edward of Lancaster at Tewkesbury. (The way they put it, you'd have thought that the Prince was about ten, and just playing with his toy soldiers.) They even went into Richard's babyhood, claiming that had lain two years in his mother's womb, and that he had been born with teeth, and hair down to his shoulders. I ask you! Who could believe such idle nonsense? It made Tegolin's tales of giants and fairies seem as prosaic as an account roll.

There was a large fire burning in the grate. It was just the place for such poisonous rubbish, and I stacked the completed volumes and the partial copies onto it, taking great pleasure in watching them catch light and begin to curl up. I'd just finished this job when I became aware of a furtive movement in the adjoining chamber. I snatched up my gonne and slow-match and pushed the dividing curtain aside. There, clutching a gilded box in his hands, was John Morton, Bishop of Ely! I'd thought he was with Buckingham, but the little toad had abandoned his new friend, and slipped back to Brecon with the intention of covering his own tracks. (I found out later that Buckingham was bogged down somewhere near Weobley, unable to get his army across into England because of the floods, and equally unable to hold it together. Morton was not the only deserter by any means, although I suspect that he was one of the first.)

"All right, Morton," I said. "My finger's kind of itchy on this slow-match. One false move and I'll fill you so full of lead that they'll not know whether to bury you or weigh you in for scrap."

"I am a Bishop," he cried, as if I needed to be reminded of the fact. "Kill me and you'll burn in hell for all eternity."

I grinned at him. "At least I'd have the satisfaction of knowing that you were already there waiting for me," I said coldly. "You forget. The King's reward will make me a very rich lady, well able to afford enough pardons from Rome to line my coffin. Put that box down, real slow, and then place your hands where you wear your mitre."

He did exactly as I said. It's amazing how obedient people become when they've got a gonne pointing at them.

"My child," he simpered, trying the soft soap, "is it not possible that we can cut a deal together? The Lord Henry Tudor knows how to value an intelligent woman. You should not allow personal animosity to stand in the way of your future career possibilities."

"You are not dealing with a mug like Buckingham now," I snapped. "God knows how you conned him into supporting that clown, but you'll not con me. You're going for a little ride to London, and a nice long talk with the King or, more likely, with his representatives. The ones who wear black hoods and undertake minor surgery."

"I'm surprised that you're so zealous in the service of a King who has murdered his own nephews. Richard will never be able to rebuild his image after such a crime. As the tale spreads, and grows in the telling, more and more will turn from him. Buckingham saw that, and grabbed the chance to go with the tide. He will not be the last."

"The boys are safe and sound," I said, "despite your efforts, Bishop. What profit is there for Richard in killing them? They are bastards, incapable of any inheritance, let alone that of the crown."

"They are dead," he snorted. "Who has not heard of the secret burial within the Tower?"

"You've started to believe in your own propaganda, you idiot. Think about it! Your version doesn't make sense. Kill a deposed king and the first thing you do is put his body on public display so that everyone can see that he's really dead. What you do not do is bury him in secret and leave a mystery. That's the way to be plagued with impostors and madmen for the next twenty years."

I saw a strange expression cross Morton's face, and realised my mistake. I should have left him in his ignorance. Until that minute he had genuinely believed that the Princes were dead, taken out by the poisoned sweetmeats planted by his accomplices. Morton, assuming that Richard had been stupid enough to hush up the murders, had taken advantage of the official silence. It had left him free to put the blame on the King, where most people would naturally expect it to lie.

He let out a sudden cry of pain, and clutched at his chest. I thought that his heart had burst, for he was past sixty, fat, and rather red in the face, but as I hesitated he sprang forward and knocked me sideways, heading for the door behind me. I had not stopped rolling over when I discharged my piece at his retreating back. There was an almighty bang and a yelp as the ball grazed him, and I was left coughing and choking in the smoke. I think I used a hint too much powder.

Guy came at a run. He saw me lying on the floor and thought that I'd blown my head off.

"Have you caught him? Morton?" I demanded.

"No, my lady. Didn't know he was here."

"You must have passed him on the stairs."

"Didn't pass anyone."

Vaughans were crowding into the room, attracted by the noise.

"Anyone seen a bishop?" I asked.

For some reason, they all seemed to think that this was hilariously funny.

"Get after him!" I cried. "Bishop Morton of Ely, the King's great rebel and traitor. The King will pay a fortune for him, dead or alive. Preferably dead."

They hurried out of the room even faster than they had come, inspired by the thought of all that gold. But we never did catch him. I can only think that he made use of a secret passage, or that there was some well-concealed room where he was able to hide until we had all gone away.

I left Brecon in the midst of a party of very happy Vaughans. There was a huge amount of booty, including Buckingham's two young daughters, and the castle blazed fiercely behind us. I entertained the hope that Morton was still inside.

I carried the gilded box that the Bishop had left behind in his haste. It contained some intriguing correspondence. At last I had Margaret Beaufort bang to rights.

XI

They found Buckingham hiding on a tenant's farm near Wem in Shropshire. Unfortunately for him, he had not been a very supportive landlord over the years, and the man concerned had no qualms about handing him over to the Sheriff, who in turn gave him into the care of James Tyrell.

Buckingham was taken to Salisbury, where the King was lodged after crushing the other wings of the rebellion. The trial was brief. Very brief. It was only really a matter of formality before they struck his head off. Richard refused to see the prisoner or to hear his pleas for pardon.

So much for Buckingham.

Several gentlemen of the South were executed. Sir George Browne was one of them. He had led the revolt in Kent, and I'm pleased to say that one of my many nephews, Lord Cobham, was responsible for blasting him out of Bodiam Castle. (A pretty place, Bodiam, by the way. I recommend a visit if you're ever in that neck of the woods. It rates three Fetterlocks for comfort.)

Richard pardoned many other offenders, but there were those who trusted him so little that they preferred to flee abroad. Morton's propaganda had been very effective.

(I must admit that I had some embarrassing family trouble as a result of this revolt. My brother Thomas, who should have known better, got himself mixed up in it, and I had to arrange for a pardon for him. Suspicion also fell on my eldest brother, Audley, but fortunately he was able to clear himself and remained part of Richard's governing team.)

Henry Tudor sailed into Poole Harbour with his invasion fleet, but he was cautious, and somehow figured out that the fellows lining the shore were Richard's men and not, as they pretended, his own supporters. (I suspect that they cheered too loudly and aroused his suspicions.) He shot off back to France as fast as the wind could blow him.

Back at Westminster, I was summoned into Richard's presence. He had the correspondence I had captured spread out all over his desk, and was wearing a look of satisfaction that was dangerously close to a smile.

"A fine piece of work, Alianore," he said, rising and pouring out a glass of wine for me with his own hands.

I shrugged. "It was pretty straightforward."

He gestured at the papers. "I can't believe they didn't encipher any of this."

"They're just clever amateurs, Your Grace. Though it's a great pity that Morton escaped, since we could certainly have nailed him for treason and attempted murder."

He nodded. "We'll attaint him in any event. Lovel has a report that he's turned up in Flanders. Odd that he should go there instead of joining Tudor. Perhaps he hopes to stir up trouble for us in Calais."

"There is, of course, still Margaret Beaufort. These papers prove beyond doubt that she was hand in hand with the turd Morton in all this. The conspiracy with Buckingham, the attempts on your nephew's lives, and more ..."

Richard sat back in his big chair and twisted his rings. "Yes," he acknowledged, "I've read your report, and some of the facts in it astonish me. How any lady of royal descent could involve herself in such work I do not know. However, the fact remains that I can't execute her. It's contrary to the Knightly Code except in cases of husband-murder, and that's one of the few crimes she hasn't committed. Moreover, I can't inflict disgrace upon Lord

Stanley. I know you don't like him. Nor do I, but he's served me loyally throughout this little squall."

He saw me grit my teeth, and added, "Margaret will not go unpunished. Her lands will be forfeited, though they'll be granted to Stanley for life so that he's not the loser thereby. She'll be deprived of her own servants and imprisoned, in her husband's custody, for the rest of her life. That will put an end to her conspiracies."

"Unless," I pointed out, "she involves Stanley in them."

He nodded. "Stanley's loyalty has been tested, and did not fail. This is a further test. However much he slips and slides, he'll not be able to escape the responsibility for Margaret's future conduct."

I nodded. It was shrewd to give Stanley enough rope to hang himself, and yet at the same time every opportunity and encouragement to stick with us.

"And now, what of you, Alianore?" he asked. "What recompense do you wish to claim?"

"I am content to be nothing more than the Queen's waiting-woman and Roger Beauchamp's wife," I said. "I seek no reward for myself. I couldn't have done anything at Brecon without the Vaughans. They should benefit from Your Grace's favour. My servant, Guy Archer, would appreciate a few additions to his collection of gold coins. And for my husband's services, if you can see your way clear, I suggest a small grant of land. Nothing too fancy. Half a dozen forfeited manors or so. I've always liked Kent, especially in the summer."

"Granted," said Richard, so quickly that I knew at once that I'd not asked for enough.

Still, with the new manors we were very rich indeed.

The Parliament that met in January passed an Act called Titulus Regius, which confirmed Richard's right to the crown in terms that should have put any remotely sensible man out of doubt. The rebels were attainted, of course, but the rest of the legislation dwelt too much on the rights of the common people. The common people are all very well in their place, but when the chips are down it's no use looking for them on the battlefield unless some lord, knight or gentleman has taken the trouble to fetch them with him. Richard was buttering the wrong parsnips, and the lawyers, who are never happy with any Parliament that does not fatten their purses, grumbled mightily.

It was not long after this that Elizabeth Woodville came to terms with the King and emerged from Westminster Sanctuary with her tail of daughters. She had been sorely beguiled by Margaret Beaufort and Bishop Morton, and we were now in a position to prove this even to her satisfaction. Not that that prevented her from asking Richard for additional safeguards, including a public oath of his good intentions.

Dame Elizabeth Grey, as we all had to learn to call her, retired to the country with her younger daughters and a pension of seven hundred marks a year, which was certainly enough to keep even an ex-Queen in hennins. The eldest girls, Elizabeth and Cecily of York, were deposited at Court, in Anne's care.

"Gorgeous, aren't they?" asked Roger, as we watched them dancing on their first night back in circulation.

"Don't get any ideas," I said, warningly, "or you could have a very nasty accident with my knife."

He was right, though. They were gorgeous, even in the shabby gowns they wore before the King got around to making proper provision for them. Cecily took after her mother, and gave you an idea of what that beautiful lady must have looked like as a girl, while Elizabeth of York, or Bessy as everyone called her, was tall and fair and just a little plump around the face. Oddly enough she reminded me of a young Anne Neville, both in figure and feature, and this is not so hard to explain when you bear in mind how very closely they were related. However, looks can be deceptive. Anne was always practical and ambitious, as well as downright clever.

Bessy lived in a dream, and just went where the tide took her, without fuss or complaint.

We remained at Westminster until March. Anne was now quite ill, there was no doubt of it. There was no strength in her and sometimes, when she coughed, she brought up blood. Her waist was as slender as that of a starved weasel, and she had herself laced into a corset for the fashion of it, not for constraint. The formal duties of a Queen were becoming an ordeal for her, but she had an iron will, and didn't give up, although she often collapsed as soon as she was out of public view. I swore her other women to secrecy, laying it on particularly thick with Bessy and Cecily, but I was well aware that I was wasting my time. Such things cannot be kept private for ever. I was fool enough to think that we were deceiving the King until one night when I saw his eyes on her. He knew.

There was ill news from Burgundy. Anne gave me the letter to read for myself. The Duchess wrote to say that there had been another attempt on the life of King Edward's sons, and this time it had met with partial success. Young Ned had been killed in a hunting accident that hadn't really been an accident and Dickon, fearing for his life, had fled her Court. She did not know what had happened to him.

The King said nothing, but you could see the sorrow and guilt on his face. His sister had warned him that the boys were not safe in Flanders, but with one thing and another he'd not got around to doing anything about it. He could not acquit himself of the responsibility.

I knew now why Morton had chosen Flanders as his place of exile, and I blamed myself not a little for putting him on the trail – though it was true that I had not told him where they were. He had obviously worked this out for himself.

Richard decided upon another great progress to the Midlands and the North, for we were having serious hassle with the Scots again. Anne brightened, realising that she would have a chance to visit Middleham and see her son.

Unfortunately it was not to be. We were no further north than Nottingham when a messenger arrived from Middleham, clad in mourning. The Prince had died, suddenly, and in agony.

Richard and Anne locked themselves up in a room for two days, draining their tears in privacy. How they contrived to comfort each other I shall never know, for they were both near mad with grief, but when they emerged they wore calm, fixed expressions, and made polite conversation with the rest of us.

"I must bear my lord another son," Anne told me, when we were next alone together. She was quite calm about it, as if it was no more than a matter of ordering a cheese from the local market.

"You almost died over Edward," I pointed out, "and that was nearly eight years ago. You were told then that you must have no more."

"One way or another, my life is over," she snapped. "You have skill with herbs, Alianore. I command you to help me."

"I cannot work miracles even for Your Grace," I said, for two of us could play at the game of being formal.

"Then kill me. Let me make way for someone who can give Richard the heir he needs. You would only be speeding up the work of nature."

"I have never poisoned anyone in my life," I told her, "and I am certainly not going to start with you. If Richard wishes to be rid of you he has ample grounds for divorce. You should have had a dispensation for your marriage in the first place, being such close cousins. Ask him to write to the Pope if that's what you want. I doubt very much whether he will take you up on your offer."

I knew he wouldn't. If anything he clung to her more than ever, and brought in the very best of physicians in an attempt to restore her to health. These fellows poured all manner of filth down Anne's throat, but it did no good.

Anne, of course, was right. Setting aside all sentiment, Richard needed an heir. To be without one was a serious weakness. The one available to him was their nephew, Warwick, George's son by Isabel, who was far too slow of wit to be considered suitable.

Richard struck a deal with Brittany by which, in return for our help in defending them from the French, plus the revenues from the earldom of Richmond, they would hand over Henry Tudor. Someone warned Tudor, and he managed to escape into France, not an hour too soon.

Elizabeth Woodville wrote to her eldest son by Lord Grey, the Marquis of Dorset, to come home from exile and make his peace with the King. This was a great boost to us, but, unfortunately, Dorset was captured by Tudor's agents and made prisoner before he could leave France.

It was obvious that we had a serious security leak. I suspected Stanley, and I know that Lovel had him watched closer than ever, but to no avail.

Christmas was soon upon us, and Bessy and Cecily were provided with more new clothes, and of the very best, as if they were Richard's own daughters. Moreover, as the festivities went on, Bessy and the Queen took advantage of their similar build, combined their wardrobes, and amused themselves by changing gowns with each other about every half hour. I know this because it was my job to help them, and I got a bit sick of it.

Courts are strange places for rumours. Before long word was abroad that Richard had made Bessy his mistress, and that she was to become Queen as soon as he had found a way to rid himself of Anne.

Richard and Anne could not win. This was their reward for treating their nieces with love and honour and kindness. Perhaps it would have been better to dress the girls in rags and set them to work in the kitchens. At least then the criticisms would have been well founded.

Anne had tried every trick she knew to get with child, and I helped her as best I could by dosing her with the appropriate potions, but it was hopeless. She was dying, and all we could do was watch. Her physicians told Richard that he could no longer sleep with her, for fear of infection, and this broke her heart, for it deprived her of her last faint chance of giving him a son. She seemed to shrink, day by day.

She died at last on the 16th March, and the sky darkened as she passed, for there was a total eclipse of the sun at that very hour. Westminster is a gloomy palace at the best of times, and the eclipse cast some very strange shadows. It seemed to me for an instant that I caught a glimpse of the Kingmaker in the crowd around the Queen's bed, watching with sad eyes. It must have been a trick of the light.

Richard was cursed with ill luck. That eclipse was a natural event, as any man with a shred of learning will accept, and would have occurred whether Anne had died on that day or not. But you cannot explain such difficult concepts to the ignorant and the unlettered. They saw it as proof positive that he had poisoned her.

I have just had to break off writing again to deal with Sir Humphrey Berkeley. The fellow is becoming something of a bore, expecting hospitality at all manner of inconvenient times. He professes to be sorely hurt by my husband's claim that he is in unlawful possession of some of our cattle. He suggests that the only balm for his wounded honour is Constance's hand in marriage, with five hundred marks in dowry to go with her.

In the old days Roger would have ridden round to Berkeley's joint with a few stout fellows, rearranged the furniture rather substantially, and smeared the insolent rogue's innards all over the courtyard. One has to be slightly more subtle in these degenerate times, especially when one is tied up in Mr Tudor's web of parchment bonds and suspended penalties. No wonder the damned lawyers are all waxing so fat.

I don't much care to be threatened under my own roof, however obliquely. Berkeley is blissfully unaware that I have broken my fast on bigger and better men, and spat out the bones. He has much to learn, and if he's not very careful he'll be going to church for his funeral rather than his wedding.

All this talk about death reminds me that I must go down to the church to see how the workmen are getting on with our tomb – mine and Roger's, that is. We decided to place an order well in advance, because you can't trust the young ones to look after these matters once you've gone. You're quite likely to end up under one of those cheap, ghastly brass plates that you see all over the Cotswolds.

A little man came out to us from Bristol with his catalogue. He could knock you out a standard Knight with a Moustache and a Lion at His Feet for next to nothing. Apparently he bought up a whole load of bankrupt stock a few years ago, and has got the things stacked up in piles in his back shed. Good value I suppose, if you don't mind posterity thinking that you used to wear your grandfather's armour.

I insisted on a proper alabaster job, with full portraiture and heraldry. Our effigies will each wear Richard's White Boar livery badge, and our hands should really be raised in two-fingered salute to Henry Tudor. Unfortunately, the mason said that that was against his guild rules, and so Roger and I will lie there with his hand clasped on mine, holding it down.

This little lot is going slap bang in the middle of the chancel, so people are not going to forget us. We need a few prayers. Doesn't everyone? To give an added boost to my hopes of salvation, I've put in a fancy new window down the road at Hailes Abbey, with a picture of me kneeling in the corner to make sure that God doesn't forget who paid for it. Not even Henry Tudor can take that away from me.

Six days after Anne's death, Richard despatched an embassy to the King of Portugal, proposing his own marriage to the Princess Joanna, and offering Bessy as a bride to the King's cousin, the Duke of Beja.

You may think that this was a tad on the early side, but you must remember that negotiations of this kind take many months from start to finish, and that Richard was desperate for an heir. You can't just send off for a princess on Friday morning and have her warming your bed on Monday night. It doesn't work like that. It's not like sending someone to market to buy a horse.

But what, you may ask, about the familiar tale that Richard intended to marry Elizabeth of York?

The familiar tale is another foul Tudor lie. Or, to be fair, a Tudor distortion of the truth.

The fact is that Bessy fancied Richard something rotten. She set her hennin at him almost from the first, and even wrote to the Duke of Norfolk asking him to help promote her marriage plans. I must stress that Anne was still alive at this point.

John Howard brought the letter to me. Jocky – everyone called him that, from the King down – was a stout old lion, afraid of nothing, but this sort of business was not really in his line.

"Perhaps," he murmured, wriggling like a man with bellyache, "you can have a word in her shell-like."

"This letter is gonne-powder," I gasped, after a hurried reading. "If word of this reached Richard, the excrement would go flying from the trebuchets! If I were you, Jocky, I'd lock this up in a drawer somewhere at Framlingham, and make bloody sure no one sets eyes on it for the next century."

"You'll speak to her, then?"

I thrust the letter back into his hand. He knew as well as I did that I didn't have any choice in the matter.

I have had some lousy jobs in my life, and this was one of the lousiest. Bessy was a lovely girl, with not an ounce of malice in her, and I had to walk right into her dreams and shatter them.

"There was a prophecy," she said, quite matter-of-factly, "that I shall be Queen of England. I never understood how that could be, until Richard took the throne. Now I see."

"You see wrongly," I snapped. We were in the gloomiest window-embrasure in Westminster. You could look out over the Thames and watch the sparkling turds and dead cats floating by on their way down to London. "These prophecies are two a penny, and don't mean a damn. What joker came up with this one?"

"An old Welshwoman," she answered, her blue eyes shining. "She came to me in the garden at Eltham, when I was just a little girl. She had a funny name. Teg something. I wasn't frightened. She just took my hand, and looked at it, and said what would come, and then she vanished, while my back was turned. It was like a dream, but it wasn't a dream, honestly it wasn't."

"Bessy," I sighed, "come down to earth, dear. The King is your uncle. He can't marry you. Not without one hell of a dispensation, anyway. What would he gain if he did? Parliament has declared you a bastard. You've no inheritance and no dowry. He's already suspected of poisoning the Queen to make way for you, and if he was idiot enough to take you as his wife he'd confirm those suspicions and alienate all his northern supporters, who love Anne Neville because she's the Kingmaker's daughter. The only possible advantage he'd gain by marrying you would be to deny you to that clown Henry Tudor, but he can just as easily achieve that end by giving you to someone else."

She stood up, tears forming in her beautiful eyes. "You're forgetting one thing," she sniffed. "I love Richard. And Richard loves me. We shall be married. And when I become Queen, my first business will be to banish you from the Court."

You will scarcely credit this, but the fool went straight from me to Richard, and declared her love. The subsequent explosion was heard in Ipswich and Reading.

This was why Bessy was tacked on to the Portuguese proposal, and why she and Cecily were sent off to live at Sheriff Hutton. Despite this the lying rumours continued to spread around the Court, and around London, until Richard was forced to make a public statement to the effect that he had not murdered his wife and that he had no intention of marrying Elizabeth of York. However, to this very day, there are still people who are sufficiently stupid to believe the contrary.

XII

Now that Anne was dead I no longer had any official position at Court, but Francis Lovel was short of staff and had urgent need of my assistance on the Intelligence side, and I was required to stay on to help with the collation of the numerous reports we had coming in from our people in France. It was clear now that Tudor intended to invade us during the summer. We even had an indication that his intended point of landing would be Milford, near Southampton, and Lovel and my brother John, Lord Audley, Treasurer of England, were sent to those parts to organise the naval defences and put the local punters into a state of readiness.

Richard's followers were put on alert. Jocky Howard and his son were ready to mobilise the men of East Anglia at a moment's notice, and Northumberland was under instruction to hold the North in readiness. For Lancashire and Cheshire we had to rely on slippery Stanley and his younger brother, Sir William, neither of whom I would have trusted beyond the end of my darning needle. I reckoned that the best we could hope for was that they'd stand by as neutrals, which was their usual form, and the reports we had in from the few reliable agents in those parts tended to confirm me in that view.

Roger was quite looking forward to the battle. He'd ordered a new set of armour for the occasion, and was itching to try it out. He came clanking into our solar at Horton Beauchamp.

"You're getting a bit old for this sort of thing," I reminded him. "I don't want you taking any silly chances. Leave the heroism to the younglings – they deserve their career opportunities. Stay with the King, in the command position, where you'll be safe."

He swung his war-hammer in an experimental arc, and smashed the top off a jug of wine we had standing on the dresser.

"Sorry about that," he said, sheepishly. His voice was muffled by the closed sallet he was wearing on his head.

"How many times have I asked you not swing your battle-axe in the house?" I cried. "You'll be setting up a quintain on my bed next!"

He opened the visor. "It's not a battle-axe, it's a war-hammer," he pointed out, as if that made any difference.

"Have you any idea how many herbs I have to mix together to get red wine out of the carpet? Let me get you out of this pile of scrap."

Every young damosel should be taught how to arm a man, and how to take the harness off again. After all, it'd be jolly inconvenient if you were trapped in a cave with your knight, with a fierce dragon outside, and you didn't know how to fit your protector into his armour. He can't do it all himself, he has to have either an esquire or a lady to help, and in my experience there's never an esquire around when you really need one. It's no use calling on some old peasant who happens to be passing. He won't have been trained for the work, and you've no more right to expect him to do your job than he has to expect you to do his.

You never appreciate how many separate pieces make up a man's war harness until it's all spread out over your solar floor.

"That was pretty quick," said Roger approvingly, watching the sands still running through the quarter-hour glass. "Must have been pretty close to your personal best."

"Not bad," I agreed, "bearing in mind that I'm out of practice."

"This will probably be the last battle of our lifetime," he predicted. "Once Tudor's dead, there'll be no one left to give Richard hassle, and England will be at peace. That's why I have to be there."

"There'll be other battles," I told him. "Richard has the French next on his list, and they know it. That's why Anne de Beaujeu is supporting Tudor."

"Strange crowd, the French," he muttered. "Fancy having a woman as Regent! Whatever next!"

"She's very shrewd," I pointed out, "and that's one of the things that worries me. Remember that she's old King Lewis's daughter, and he was the cleverest bastard in Europe. He'd not have left his country in her care without being certain that she could cut mustard."

"Are you trying to tell me that this Tudor fellow is a serious threat?"

I shrugged. "I don't know. I do know that my father died because he underestimated the enemy, and I don't want you to follow suit."

"It should be a fairly straightforward piece of fighting," he opined. "Not nearly as bad as Barnet or Tewkesbury, and absolutely nothing on Towton. Now, that was a battle! Fought in a snowstorm so thick you could scarcely see the end of your arm. We walked the horses over Lancastrian corpses all the way to York, and finished with a really first-class round of executions."

"Roger," I said, patiently, "I do wish that you would stop being nostalgic for the good old days. All I can remember is that you were almost killed at Tewkesbury, and that some of us had to spend six months mopping the sweat from your brow and carrying you to the garderobe. I want you to keep your eyes open for treachery, and don't be afraid to run away if the day is lost. I'll not think any the less of you."

"I don't like all this defeatist talk, Alianore," he snapped, frowning. "Have you had a premonition or something? I thought you had more sense than to go scrying for the future in candle flames."

I felt a cold dribble of sweat run down my belly. I hadn't touched a Tarot card in years, or looked for shapes in the smoke, but I was uncomfortable about the battle that was to come, as if someone was constantly whispering a warning in my ear.

"There's going to be treachery," I said. "I can feel it."

"The Stanleys?"

"Yes."

He snorted. "Don't worry. Richard will have come up with a few surprises for those sods." His eyes fixed on me, and ran up and down, an idea forming in his head. He strolled across to the window and opened the casement, then shouted for Guy, who was supervising the archery practice in the courtyard. (You can't leave the young men to it these days, or they just go off to play football or drink cider. I don't know what the world is coming to.)

"Yes, Sir Roger?" Guy called back.

"Any sign of a messenger from the King?"

"No, Sir Roger."

"Sure?"

"Absolutely."

"If one does happen to arrive, keep him quiet for half an hour, will you?"

"Only half an hour?" I protested.

"Wife," he grunted, "sacrifices have to be made in time of war. Turn round, and let me see how quickly I can unlace your gown."

A week or so later we were at Nottingham with the King. Richard hadn't mustered his forces as he was awaiting sure news of Tudor's landing. It's damned expensive to keep thousands of soldiers hanging around for weeks in idleness, and no English king has ever been able to afford such a luxury as a standing army. (The French keep one, but their people are crippled with taxation to pay for it. You'd never get away with that sort of thing in this country.)

At last word arrived of Tudor's landing. It was in a far corner of Wales, on the shores of Milford Haven. Our agents in France had obviously not realised that there was more than one Milford!

We were not unduly alarmed. To reach London Tudor was going to have to march through the territories controlled by the Vaughans and their kinsman, William Herbert, Earl of Huntingdon, who was wedded to Richard's bastard daughter, Katherine. We knew that he would struggle to get through that little barrier.

But then reports began to arrive that Tudor was moving north, along the coast. We could not make out where he was going, although a captured letter, directed to Stanley and pleading abjectly for assistance, made most amusing reading. Instead of keeping it in the Intelligence Office, Richard had it passed around the top table at suppertime so we could all have a good laugh.

Lord Stanley had sent word that he was ill, confined to his bed at Lathom with the Sweating Sickness. This disease is often fatal, but I had the peculiar feeling that Stanley would make a full recovery when the time was ripe. Richard obviously had the same feeling, because he had Stanley's eldest son, George, Lord Strange, with us at Nottingham, and was not at all inclined to let him go home to Lancashire.

Strange gave you the distinct impression that he was the nervous sort. (He was not Margaret Beaufort's son, by the way, but the product of Stanley's first marriage, which was to one of the Kingmaker's many sisters.) You only had to drop your eating knife on the tiles and he would jump three feet.

I'd have bet my last set of garters that Strange would try to escape, and doubled up on the chance that he'd make a cock of it. I'd have won on both counts, because the rope of sheets that he used broke in half, and he fell about twenty feet onto solid rock, shattering his ankle. He was damned lucky not to break his fool neck.

Richard was too old-fashioned to allow ladies in the torture-chamber. I can't vouch for the details of what happened next, but I was given sight of the transcript, and it's fair to say that Strange didn't need much in the way of seed before he began to sing.

He admitted that he, with his uncle, Sir William, and his cousin Sir John Savage, had agreed to go over to Tudor. Also involved was Sir Gilbert Talbot, the High Sheriff of Shropshire, uncle to the young Earl of Shrewsbury. On the other hand, he claimed that his father was still loyal to Richard.

"What do you make of it?" the King asked me, twisting his rings.

"It stinks to high heaven," I said, putting the paper aside, "but it also makes a degree of sense. The Stanley family has always tried to keep a foot in both camps. It's exactly what they did at Blore Heath. At Tewkesbury too. Sir William was there with you, but where was his brother? Carefully absent. Sir William may fight you, but my guess is that Stanley himself will just stand off, and pretend that he was delayed on the road."

"The prospect of his son being strung up from the nearest tree may just change his mind," Richard snapped. "George Strange is guilty of treason, by his own admission, and I'll execute him if his father shows the least sign of disobedience. It seems to be the only language these people understand."

"I'd like to pay a call on Sir William, if you'll allow it," I replied. "I've an idea that I'd like to try, one that might just come off."

"I'm not sending you into his camp, Alianore. It's too dangerous. I'll settle for proclaiming him a traitor, and Savage and Talbot with him. That'll give their friends cause to have second thoughts."

"By your leave, Sire," I persisted, "I do think it's worth the risk. If we can knock Sir William out of the game, it'll mean that you only have the Tudor himself to fight, and that should be something of a doddle for you."

"What do you say, Roger?" the King asked.

My husband shrugged. "I doubt whether William Stanley, for all his faults, is the sort who would harm a lady. If Alianore has a plan that will keep him out of the battle, then I suggest you let her go for it. The alternative is to put her under lock and key for the duration."

Richard looked grim. "Very well," he agreed, "but see to it that you take no undue risks."

I took a small escort with me, which included Guy as well as one of the King's heralds. This chap went by the name of Blanc Sanglier, or Blanc for short, and was a bit of a pain, really. He insisted on stopping at every village cross to blow his trumpet and read out the proclamation that William Stanley and the rest were traitors. One can do without such delays when one is on a secret mission.

William Stanley took some tracking down, but we found him at last, camped just to the north of Stafford. I reckoned he had a good three thousand men with him, all wearing his livery of the Stag. From intelligence reports we knew that Tudor had passed through Shrewsbury, and lay only a few miles away, ready to join with the Stanley forces if that was what they intended.

The Herald blew his damned trumpet again, and began to unroll his scroll.

"For Christ's sake," I cried, "not here! Are you trying to get us all killed?"

"I enjoy a herald's immunity," he answered, rather snootily.

"*You* may do, you overdressed clown," snarled Guy, "but the rest of us don't."

"Moreover," I added, "if I were you, I'd not rely on William Stanley to stick to the finer points of the Knightly Code. He might just find it amusing to top you."

I was shown into Will Stanley's tent. He had a pot of ale in his hand, and was just in the middle of swilling it down. He was not much younger than his brother, but a good deal fleshier. A man who enjoyed his victuals, I judged.

"What's your business here, my Lady Beauchamp?" he boomed. "Come to spy on us, have you?"

"I'm an envoy from the King," I explained, handing him my Commission, "here to discuss terms."

"Terms? What terms?"

"The terms for your co-operation. Generous terms."

He roared with laughter. "From Gloucester? Do you think me mad? I've heard that he's proclaimed me traitor, and that's good enough for me."

"There may have been some misunderstanding," I said. "George Stanley, your nephew, may well have given the wrong impression about your intentions."

"Ah!" he cried, "so Strange betrayed me, did he?"

"Under torture," I explained. "Even brave men say whatever is required when they are tortured. Your nephew is inexperienced. I'm sure that allowances will be made, if you render some small show of loyalty."

He grunted, unimpressed.

"As matters stand," I said, sitting down on the stool opposite him, "if Tudor does the business you will be well sorted. After all, by proclaiming you traitor, Richard has given the impression that you've declared openly for his enemies, even though you haven't. Tudor will be obliged to reward you for that, even if you don't actually go so far as to fight for him."

He sat there, staring at me, without saying a word. I could tell I'd got him interested.

"But what if Richard wins?" I asked. "It's likely he will, you know. He'll command the larger army, and the better prepared. We've good intelligence about the sort of punters that Tudor's towing in his wake. The sweepings of French jails, mercenaries, and half-armed Welshmen. There's hardly an Englishman of note among them. If Richard comes out on top, my friend, you're in deep crap. A man who had better not allow himself to be taken alive."

He still sat there unblinking. He began to turn the point of his knife in the table, as if he was trying to sink a hole for an inkwell or something. I'd have had something to say to Roger if he'd treated our furniture like that, I can tell you.

"You can have the best of both worlds," I said. "Don't join in the battle, just watch from the flank. Wait until Tudor's line is broken, and then ride down and trample all over him. The King will then announce that he proclaimed you a traitor as a piece of trickery, and that he never doubted your loyalty for a moment. He will drive home the point by creating you Earl of Chester. How about that?"

"Very clever," admitted Sir William. He paused to examine the tip of his blade, which had obviously located a piece of deathwatch beetle or something. "Would you like a mug of ale?"

I nodded, and he poured me some. It was good, strong stuff, the previous year's October brew if I'm any judge.

"How can I trust you?" he asked.

"You don't need to. That's the point. You can't lose. If Tudor is beaten, you go in on Richard's side. In the unlikely event of Richard being beaten, you make a show of going in on Tudor's side. Or you stay out altogether if you choose. It's easy."

Stanley got to his feet, stroking his stubbly chin. I've noticed that men on campaign very rarely bother to shave. I suppose it's too much trouble to arrange for soap and hot water when you're living in a tent.

"Call me old-fashioned," he grunted, "but it'd ease my mind no end to have some little thing in the way of security."

"You have my word as a lady," I pointed out.

"A woman's word," he chuckled, "is worth precisely nothing."

"Sir," I said, coldly, "if it comes to that the word of a Stanley does not have much of an exchange rate. Do we have a deal, or do we not?"

He nodded. "We have a deal. I'll stand neutral until the battle's settled, then join the winning side. You have my word. On one condition. Before the battle I want a charter of pardon from the King, under the Great Seal."

"And he shall have it," said Richard. The tone of his voice was just the same as when he had condemned Hastings to death.

We were at the White Boar Hotel in Leicester. Richard was sitting on his great bed, and the rest of us were standing, apart from Northumberland, who thought himself grand enough to occupy the stool by the King's desk.

"Not that it will do him any good, of course," Richard went on. "After the battle I intend to execute the entire Stanley family, without distinction. I'm buggered if I'm going through all this again. Francis, where do the latest reports put them all?"

Lovel coughed. "Henry Tudor is at Atherstone, marching on London from what the scouts report. William Stanley is a little way behind him, like a shadow, somewhere between Tamworth and Atherstone. Thomas Stanley is still further to the north, holding back."

Surprise, surprise! I thought.

"He fears for Strange's head," snorted Northumberland.

"With good cause," said Richard. "Well, gentlemen, it's time to get down to talking tactics. Dame Beauchamp, you have leave to withdraw, with our thanks. I have another commission for you, but it can wait until morning."

I left them to it, wondering what the morning would bring. It would be my last commission, that was certain. This time I was absolutely determined to retire to Horton Beauchamp once the fighting was over.

It was very early indeed when Richard sent for me, but the preparations for the army to march out of Leicester were already in full swing. He paced the room, wrapped in his chamber-robe, his hands toying with a battle-axe that was nearly as big as he was.

"Alianore," he said, "I expect to win this battle. If I were a betting man, which I'm not, I'd say that our chance of victory was about eight to one on. So, this is in the way of a precaution."

He handed me a sealed document, and a purse heavy with gold.

"In the event of my defeat, you will proceed to Sheriff Hutton. It is essential that the Ladies Elizabeth and Cecily of York do not fall into the hands of this Welsh mountebank. A ship will be waiting at Scarborough to take them, and you, to my sister in Flanders. On the other hand, if I manage to thrash Tudor and his chums, you can tear up the commission and keep the gold for yourself. You have more than earned it."

In the event of your defeat, I thought, I shall have a few problems of my own to sort out, without troubling myself with the arrangements for a trip to the Continent. However, one does not say things like that to one's King. I curtsied, and promised that he could rely on me to do my best.

XIII

It's very difficult for me to describe the Battle of Bosworth, for the simple reason that I wasn't there. I refuse to introduce fiction into this Chronicle by pretending that I watched it from a tree or something, as some say Owain Glyndwr watched the Battle of Shrewsbury. However, I've spoken to many men who were on the battlefield from start to finish. As their accounts all differ in detail, and often in substance, I am content that my version of the truth is as reliable as anyone else's, and certainly more accurate than anything published by Henry Tudor.

Richard was the first to arrive, and he selected the site of the battlefield. There was a big, deep marsh protecting the front of his position, which meant that Tudor and his friends could not make a direct attack.

Tudor's vanguard, under the Earl of Oxford, marched around the edge of this soft ground until they made contact with Richard's vanguard, led by old Jocky Norfolk. The fighting then kicked off, and pretty fierce it was too, but the greater part of both armies could do no more than stand by and watch – they had the marsh between them, remember?

Poor Jocky was killed early doors, but his son, Thomas Howard, Earl of Surrey, who was past forty and a good soldier, was still doing the business. There was no need for panic. Not on our side, anyway.

William Stanley was some way off to the north, well able to observe what was going on, but evidently disinclined to do anything about it. There was no marsh between him and Richard, although there was sloping ground that he would have needed to climb to make an attack. He just stayed where he was, waiting to see which way it went. His brother, Lord Stanley, was even further off, a good five miles away or more. There was no way that he was going to intervene, that was the one certainty of the day.

At this point Richard sent Roger to Northumberland, who was in charge of our rearguard. Northumberland was ordered to go around the other end of the marsh, so that the Tudor army would find Yorkists attacking it from two different directions. I think this is called a pincer movement, or something of that sort.

Northumberland has often been accused of treachery by bitter Yorkists. Although he was no particular friend of mine, I must be fair and say that this is a very harsh verdict. The lie of the land was such that he just did not know what was going on as far as the main battle was concerned. However, he was very well placed to keep an eye on William Stanley's forces, as he had been told to do, and he argued that he needed to carry on doing just that.

He was still discussing this point with Roger when things began to go horribly wrong. Henry Tudor broke from his army, and began to ride northwards, towards William Stanley. I can only think that he was minded to beg Stanley for assistance. If he was running away he was headed in the wrong direction, and if he was confident of victory he had no need to go anywhere.

Tudor had only a few men as escort, and Richard saw his chance to take him out. He gathered the mounted knights of his household around him, and charged down the slope towards Tudor, who was, I suppose, about a quarter of a mile away. The rest of his division of the army, lacking orders, were left scratching their helmets.

Richard was ill-advised to risk his own life at such a crucial moment, but I dare say the sight of Tudor, who was riding under the banner of a king of England, wound him up to some tune. It is, moreover, easy to be wise after the event. If Richard had succeeded, however narrowly, the battle would have been won, and he would have reigned in peace for years. As it was, he came very close to victory. Close enough to kill the giant of a man who was carrying Tudor's banner. I suspect that Mr Tudor was very much in need of a change of armour at this point.

But then, of course, William Stanley and his men put in their groat's worth. In all the confusion I doubt whether they were certain of what they were doing, with, as I said, two identical royal banners and – in their armour – two fairly identical kings in the middle of it all.

Richard was hacked down. His last words, as reported to me, were: "Treason, treason, treason!"

Was it treason? Was it a mistake? I don't know.

My old friend Rob Percy was among those killed with the King. So were Richard Ratcliffe and Robert Brackenbury, and many other decent fellows whose names have not intruded into this Chronicle.

The battle was over. There's no point in hanging around once your leader is dead. If you do, you've a good chance of hanging around one of the local trees until your bones drop apart. That's what happened to William Catesby, who was captured. I'm pleased to say that Roger did what any sensible man would have done in the circumstances. He waved goodbye to Northumberland, and fled the field.

I was back at Leicester, at the White Boar, sorting through the latest intelligence reports. My first inkling that something was wrong was when the landlord went up a ladder with a pot of blue paint, and started to make some subtle changes to his inn sign. It seemed an odd time to decide that the place needed a new image.

Then the fugitives began to arrive, in ones and twos at first. Francis Lovel was among them, and he went to the trouble of calling in to tell me to get the hell out of town. I asked him if he was quite certain that we were beaten. After all, some Yorkists ran all the way from Barnet to London back in 1471, crying defeat, and were left very red-faced when it transpired that King Edward had turned things around and won the day.

"Richard is dead," he said, miserably, "it's as certain as that."

I cannot begin to describe how horrified I was, so I won't bother to try.

"Help me destroy the Intelligence papers," I pleaded. "We mustn't allow them to fall into the hands of the enemy."

There were only the live records at Leicester, of course. (The archives were back at Nottingham Castle.) We started to burn them, down in the kitchen, but it was a hopeless task. There were too many of them, and we only succeeded in stifling the fire. In the end we borrowed a cart from the landlord, loaded it up as best we could, and tipped the papers into the River Soar.

I must admit that I kept a few choice documents back, for insurance purposes, and Francis Lovel left with a few more stuffed into his saddlebags. My selection included one real peach I had uncovered during my rootings at Westminster, a file of Hastings' that had never been indexed, but which Richard, on grounds of chivalry, had forbidden me to publish. Chivalry is a luxury that you can afford when you're on the winning side, but when you're pinned to the ground, and there's a knife at your throat, you jolly well have to land your kicks where you can.

It was then that Roger arrived. I don't think I have ever been so relieved to see anyone in my life.

"Get me out of this damned harness," he barked impatiently. "It's time to go. The neighbours are about ten yards from my behind."

I think it's fair to say that we slipped out of the north gate of Leicester at about the same time that Tudor and his sordid gang of foreigners and traitors marched in from the west. They brought Richard's body with them, naked and slung over a horse, as if they were anxious to demonstrate that they didn't have any manners. I'm glad that I wasn't around to see it.

My son Harry has brought eternal disgrace upon the proud name of Beauchamp. Having wasted some five years at University, he has come home at last and announced, bold as brass, that he now wishes to become a cursed lawyer! I don't know what his father will say. A man has a right to expect better from his own flesh and blood.

The influence of Harry's friend, Geoffrey Archer, is much to blame. Geoffrey, Guy's eldest son, went to University with Harry, when they were both fifteen, to act as his servant and to study at our expense, so that he might one day serve us in some useful capacity such as steward or priest. However, boys get into bad company at Oxford, and Geoffrey developed an interest in the law. This was no great shame in him. He is, after all, the son of an archer, and has his way to make in the world. Harry has no such excuse. He should seek out a respectable troop of mercenaries to join. There's always a war somewhere to provide a gentleman with honourable employment.

Still, it's good to have all my boys home again.

Thomas takes life rather seriously, as befits his father's heir, but he is a fine jouster, and would make a great and worthy knight if he had a half decent king to serve, instead of a snivelling, shuffling, Welsh accounts clerk. As for Rick, he has always been the scapegrace of the family, and although he has settled down somewhat since we found him a place in his cousin Audley's household, he much prefers to idle around at home, swiving, boozing, and seeking mischief. He openly names my nephew Audley a fool, and speaks of finding himself a better master, but he's far too lazy to do more than talk about it.

My sons have their faults, but they are close to each other as fingers on a hand, and don't quarrel among themselves like many brothers I could mention. Geoffrey Archer is like another link in the chain, and the four of them treat Constance like a princess, which is exactly what the girl does not need. I'd never have learned to stand on my own feet if I'd had brothers like that. No wonder she has a head full of silly notions. Her tears have incensed them against Humphrey Berkeley, and I just hope that their father gets home before things get out of hand.

Constance is absurdly quiet. She sits mending one of Thomas's shirts. Suddenly, her big blue eyes lock straight on me.

"Mother, I won't really have to marry Sir Humphrey, will I?" she demands.

"That's for your father to say," I tell her.

"Have I no right to say what I want?"

"Every right, so be it that you do as you are told. My brother bade me marry your father. End of story. I don't see why you should be any different."

One of the advantages of maturity is that you can bend the truth to some tune and get away with it, especially when you're dealing with your children.

As I write this my sons and Geoffrey are practising archery in our garden. I can watch them from the big window in the solar, where I have my desk. I can't imagine why they have suddenly become interested in toxophily, but they have a good teacher in Geoffrey's father, and I haven't seen many arrows off target. Guy was Champion Archer of the West of England for donkey's years. He was so good, in his prime, that you couldn't get a bet on. Not unless you could persuade him to compete under a false name, which we did manage on the odd occasion.

Guy joined Roger and me somewhere north of Leicester, as much by luck as anything else, and the three of us hurried to Nottingham, where we burnt a few more files. It was just like the old days.

We were pressed for time, of course, for we knew that Tudor's men could not be very far to our rear. It was obvious that they would want to secure Bessy as a top priority, to say nothing of her cousin, young Warwick, who was also at Sheriff Hutton. I took it upon myself to break the news to Bessy. Her shoulders shook when I described the manner of her uncle's death, but she bore up well. She was King Edward's daughter right enough. I began to speak of her aunt in Flanders, and the ship waiting at Scarborough.

"I am not going anywhere," she said, with a set of the mouth that reminded me of King Richard in a stubborn mood.

"You must," I cried. "You don't understand. Tudor's men are probably in York by now. They'll be here in a matter of hours, and they'll take you to London to be married to the obnoxious little pig. Surely exile in Flanders is preferable to that. If I were in your place, I'd slit my throat with my own hand before I'd allow the fellow within twenty feet of me, let alone in my bed."

"That wouldn't solve anything, and it certainly wouldn't bring Richard back. Have you ever heard of duty, Dame Beauchamp? Have you ever heard of fate? You see the prophecy has come true, after all. I shall be Queen, and I shall pass my father's blood to my children."

"Your son will be the most disgusting king in English history, with the possible exception of his father," I snapped. "How about that for a prophecy?"

She started to cry then, which was just the right tactic. No one could ever be angry with Bessy for very long. Sweet, helpless princesses have only that one card to play, and they play it for all it's worth, believe me.

Roger and I talked things through. Short of abducting Bessy by force – which Roger told me was definitely not on – there was nothing more we could do. There was little joy in the thought of taking young Warwick to Flanders without her. We knew that that poor boy would never make a king.

We were well up the proverbial creek, with only our tongues for paddles.

"I think we'd better make our way home to Horton Beauchamp, and wait until the heat goes down," Roger suggested.

"You ain't just whistling *Greensleeves*, honey," I nodded. "Let's hit the trail, before Tudor and his bunch of oiks start knocking on the door."

We were too late. Not that Tudor turned up in person, you understand. He wasn't gentleman enough to make it his first business to present himself to Bessy. However, he did send Sir Robert Willoughby to collect her, Warwick, and any other titbits he could snap up.

Willoughby had an expression on his face that made you think he'd made a career out of sucking lemons. He was the sort of chap who'd ask the Pope for a special dispensation before he allowed himself as much as a sly grin.

"Sir Roger and Dame Alianore Beauchamp," he drawled. "You are my prisoners. For you, the Wars of the Roses are over."

"Sir Roger and his lady are members of my household!"

It was Bessy. She was posing on the staircase, looking down at us all along the length of her nose, already practising her part as Queen of England. I'd picked up a few tricks from Elizabeth Woodville myself. Bessy had learnt the complete repertoire. I was amazed by the change in her. Willoughby shrivelled up like a little slug in a shower of salt.

"My lady, I have my orders," he protested.

Bessy took another two steps towards him. She was wearing the most expensive gown in Yorkshire, and her hair was loose, a golden stream so long and thick that she could have walked out naked in it and still maintained her modesty.

"Then you had better be careful how you carry them out," she hissed. "It would be really sad if the King were to receive a few critical comments about your behaviour, sir. Your lack of respect."

Willoughby realised that he'd forgotten to bow, and did so, very deeply. His hat fell off, because he'd forgotten about that as well.

"My understanding," he said, "is that Sir Roger Beauchamp fought against the King at Bosworth, and that his wife was a most dangerous Intelligence Agent of the Usurper Gloucester."

Bessy started to laugh. It was a beautiful laugh, and I thought it was never going to end. The castle echoed with it. Even poor Warwick, who scarcely had the wit to know a cow from a sheep, began to howl with delight.

"King Henry is so kind," she got out at last, sobbing with the anticipation of her own joke. "He must have realised that I needed cheering up. He's sent me his Court jester!"

Willoughby could only splutter. A beetroot would have looked pale pink next to his face, believe me.

"Alianore Beauchamp an intelligence agent!" Bessy roared. "Oh, God, that's so funny! It takes her all her time to carry my train without ripping the gown off my back. She was a waiting-woman to Queen Anne, you fool, and now serves me in the same capacity. As for Sir Roger, I can give you my categorical assurance that he has not been any further south than York for several weeks."

Roger and I did not fool ourselves. We were still prisoners. But, thanks to Bessy, we were not in close confinement, and we had a long journey to London ahead of us during which we could think up a few tricks. Moreover, since Guy was classed as a mere menial, we were able to send him off to Horton Beauchamp to take care of the shop. We knew he'd take the children into his own house if the worse came to the worse.

"I owe you a big one," I told Bessy. We were on our way to York, riding in the middle of what had become a very bloated company. The locals were not mad keen on Henry Tudor, but they were more than prepared to turn out for his future wife.

She shrugged. "You were Richard's faithful servants. And my father's before that. I'll do all I can for you both, and I hope it'll be enough."

"It will," I nodded. "When Tudor sets eyes on you, he'll bite all the way through his leek. You'll be able to twist him three times round your little finger."

"We'll see," she said.

I slipped a little package of documents into her hand. "In the meantime, take care of these," I requested.

"What are they? Nothing that smacks of treason against the new government, I trust?"

"A few little snippets about the Stanley family. Just hold them for me, in case I'm searched. If you hear of anything nasty happening to me, or to Roger, pray give them straight into Tudor's hands. He'll be grateful, I promise you. There's also this ..."

'This' was the gold Richard had given me. I'd kept a couple of pieces back, but the bag was too heavy, bulky and suspicious to keep on my person for very much longer.

"Put it to good use," I said. "It's amazing how reasonable people become when they've received a decent drop. Don't let anyone think that we Beauchamps are too proud to buy our freedom, because we're not."

XIV

When we reached London, Roger was arrested and lodged in the Tower. He was in good company there, with Surrey, Northumberland, and young Warwick, as well as assorted lesser men.

I was left with Bessy, who was placed at Westminster in the care of her mother. Elizabeth Woodville was back on form again, and anxious to remind everyone that she was King Edward's widow, and not, as we had established, merely his principal mistress. This suited Tudor's book, of course, because he naturally wanted Bessy to be regarded as the heiress of the House of York.

I kept my head down, and my tongue between my teeth. Every move we made was watched, although not by Henry Tudor himself. He was a distinctly laggardly suitor.

I was not impressed when he did turn up to inspect Bessy. His accent somehow combined Welsh, French, and an anxiety to be rid of both. His clothes hung awkwardly on his scrawny carcass, his red hair was thin and straggly, and he had a tight, mean mouth. You understood why he kept his lips so close when you saw his teeth, which looked as if they'd been picked out in yellow and green paint. He struck me as the sort who'd steal the pennies from the eyes of a corpse.

To make matters worse, he pulled out a harp from behind his back and sang some ghastly song. I almost crawled under the bed, but Bessy smiled, and praised him, and generally made every possible effort to please. She was good at that sort of thing. Not that it made him hasten back for more of her company, because it didn't. There is an apt, two-word description for a man like Tudor.

Ignorant is the first part. The expletive of your choice is the second.

My brother Edmund, Bishop of Rochester as he then was, paid me a visit.

"Well, Sister," he sighed, "you are in trouble, aren't you? This is the price you pay for abandoning our family's traditional loyalty to the House of Lancaster."

I pushed my embroidery aside and made room for him to sit next to me.

"Edmund," I said, "do you by any chance recall that fellow, King Edward, who gave you your bishopric? Did you not notice that he was ever-so-slightly Yorkist in sympathy? Besides, whatever Henry Tudor is, he is certainly not the senior Lancastrian heir. The King of Portugal springs to mind as one of the many with a superior claim. So don't give me any crap about your love for Lancaster. You're just going with the flow."

"Tudor is the man in possession," he grunted. "People are not bothered with obscure questions of genealogy. Parliament is certain to acknowledge his title to the throne."

"Parliament could vote me to be Queen of Sheba," I observed, "but it wouldn't make me so by right. I'd still be plain Alianore Beauchamp in the eyes of any sensible person. What's your business here? I do hope you haven't come to gloat. I can't cope with that. It might just make me regard you as my brother, rather than my spiritual father, and suggest a part of your body into which your mitre could be suitably inserted."

"I don't particularly wish to have a brother-in-law hanged for treason," he said. "It will not do anything for my career prospects under the new set-up. Believe it or not, I would rather like to help you."

"Don't be absurd!" I snorted. "How can Roger possibly be accused of treason?"

"You're obviously unaware that King Henry dates his reign from the day before Bosworth. Therefore, all who fought against him there are liable to be adjudged traitors."

"A low trick," I said, "worthy of the man, and of the company he keeps. And you are actually prepared to work for a crook like that?"

"I do not think that this line of discussion is particularly profitable. You would do well to adopt a more positive attitude, and consider how you can be of assistance to the new administration in its task of rebuilding our country. You can begin by helping to establish the whereabouts of King Edward's sons."

"Surely that's common knowledge. King Richard had them murdered."

He put on his spectacles, and made a point of consulting a paper. "That is not what you told Bishop Morton at Brecon Castle."

I shrugged. "I was lying. When you've been involved in intelligence work for a week or two, Edmund, you'll realise that the occasional lie is a necessary tool of the job."

"How do I know that you're not lying now?"

"You don't. That's what makes it interesting."

"Alianore," he tutted, "you have always been impossible. Kindly attempt to bear in mind that your husband faces attainder, the loss of all his lands, and a stretched neck. With all the refinements added in a case of treason. You do understand why this issue of the Princes is important, don't you?"

I nodded. "Tudor must be spending big money having Bessy declared legitimate again. Popes do not come cheap. But if she's legitimate, her brothers are no less, and it'd comfort his little mind no end to be quite certain that they're dead. I'd have thought he'd be digging up the Tower staircases by now. That's where rumour said Richard had them buried. Perhaps Tudor knows better."

Edmund did not answer that. He just sat there wearing an awkward expression.

"If it will help Roger's case, I'll be delighted to co-operate," I said. "The fact is that I can't tell you much that your little pals don't already know. Morton had young Ned murdered in Flanders, and Dickon ran off into hiding. I've no idea where he is now, or whether he's alive or dead, and I'm ready to swear it on any stack of relics you care to wheel through the door."

"I hope you will not repeat your slander against Bishop Morton," he warned me, shaking a finger. "He is now Chancellor of England."

"Look, Edmund," I sighed, "you have got to tell me whether it's the truth you want, or a pack of lies that will please friend Tudor. I'll give you either, or both, if it'll save Roger. In prose, or in rhyming couplets. Just say the word."

He went off in a fearful huff. I still can't understand how I managed to upset him.

I learned many useful things during my time in Yorkist Intelligence. One of them was how to remove a seal from a letter, and put it back without anyone knowing about it. You heat up a thin, sharp knife. (The sort that men use in battle to thrust through the eye of a fallen enemy is just the job.) You slide it under the wax, very, very carefully. Then, when you want to put the seal back, you apply just enough heat to melt the wax again without destroying the impression, and press it into position with your thumb.

Once you've learned the trick, it's easier to do than to describe, and you never forget the art. I've just had occasion to undertake the advanced version of the trick, which is to transfer a seal from one letter to another. In this case from a letter that Humphrey Berkeley sent to Roger about some business, to a letter which

Berkeley doesn't know that he's written. Luckily, his hand is not difficult to imitate.

Now I sit in my solar and wait, the knife close to hand in case my boys are not as subtle or as skilful as I like to think they are.

As I was riding through our park yesterday, I could not help noticing my son, Rick, busy in the long grass. I'm not quite sure who it was that he was swiving – I couldn't see much of her, apart from her knees – but I suspect it was my young laundress, Matilda. I really must have a serious word with that lad. His sort of behaviour sets a very bad example for the servants, and in any case, he should show more consideration. A good laundress is hard to find, and I don't want to go wandering around the hiring-fairs looking for another because he's put mine out of commission.

Nor do I particularly want Matilda's father hammering on my door. He's a miller, up by Stroud, a very large and red-faced chap with the sort of voice that carries to Gloucester and back. Of course, I can soon have him thrown off the manor, but not without unpleasantness, and not without Roger getting to hear of it. Rick's card is already marked in that quarter, and at one point he was sent from home for twelve months until he begged pardon. He can't really afford to cross his father again, although it'll be difficult to get this over to him.

When I reached the far north end of the park, I found that the palisade had been broken down, and there was every sign that some of our deer had been driven out, and others killed on the spot. Roger and I have never worried about the odd bit of poaching, especially if it gets a family through a winter, but this was more than that. The work of a gang. A mounted gang at that, which always means that the gentry are involved. Starving folk do not own horses.

I rode on through the gap, and found plenty of tracks beyond, with hoof prints and boot marks leading off in all directions. The most promising trail took me into Three Mile Wood, and down a steep slope onto the public road that runs through it.

Three Mile Wood is on Berkeley's land, and he neglects it sorely, and has for years. The road is much overgrown, especially in summer, so that you can scarcely force your horse through.

I visited Berkeley to see whether he had been troubled by the same scumbags, but he said not. As part of his hospitality a large venison pasty was served up, and I got the impression that he was trying to get me drunk, the amount of wine he pressed on me.

After a while he started talking about the deeds of Perkin Warbeck, the young man who has been giving friend Tudor so much grief of late.

Warbeck claims to be Richard, Duke of York. The same Dickon who fled from Margaret of Burgundy's Court all those years ago. Whether he is truly Dickon, or a mere impostor, is more than I know, and the days have gone when I would have been curious to establish the truth. Some people take the line that Dickon – if it is Dickon – has a better claim to the throne than Bessy's husband. If Bessy is legitimate, it follows that Dickon is his father's rightful heir.

Berkeley wanted to know what I thought of all this, and I told him that I was but a foolish woman, and did not dream of meddling in men's business.

"I've heard that your husband favours this Warbeck," he said, studying my face.

"That is a lie."

"I hope no such lies reach the Sheriff's ears," he murmured. "Or the King's. His Majesty is of a notably suspicious nature, and might not trouble to listen to Beauchamp's side of the tale."

He ran his dirty fingers down the length of my thigh, and I jumped to my feet, astonished.

"I've always fancied the look of you, Alianore," he announced, tilting his head to one side and grinning.

"I thought it was my daughter you wanted."

"Oh, it is. But I've a big bed. There's room enough in it for both of you. You can't beat a mixture of youth and experience."

"You've more chance of flying to the moon," I spat out. "I'd sooner die."

He did not move. He just leaned back in his big chair, and leered. "It's not your death that is in question, my lady. You see, the rumours are not just a matter of tongues clacking. I've certain papers in my possession that could prove most embarrassing to your husband. Of course, as long as the friendship between our families is maintained – and deepens – those papers will remain safely hidden. But if you spurn the hand of friendship, I'm afraid I shall have no choice but to do my duty as a loyal subject. There will, I regret, be unfortunate consequences when the King discovers that Sir Roger has been intriguing with the impostor Warbeck. But you will only have yourself to blame."

"You're bluffing," I said. "You can't produce papers that don't exist."

"Try me. Whom do you think the King will believe? A man who bore arms against him at Bosworth? Or one who fought for him?"

He stood up, and began to walk towards me, slavering like a hungry dog that's had a meat pie held under its nose for ten minutes. "I think it's time to cement our family alliance, Alianore," he said. "Let me help you out of those uncomfortable clothes."

I don't know how I stopped myself from puking all over his carpet.

"I'm expected home," I told him. "My sons know that I'm here, and it'd be more than a tad inconvenient if they came looking for me. Ride over to Horton Beauchamp. Tomorrow. After noon. Come alone. Bring some proof of what you say. I'll make sure that

I'm on my own, and that we'll not be disturbed. We may as well make a proper job of it. Take time, and enjoy ourselves."

He hesitated, just for a moment. Then nodded. "Very well. I admit that there'll be a certain spice in cuckolding Beauchamp in his own bed. Don't disappoint me, though, will you?"

"Definitely not," I promised. "You'll never be closer to heaven. I give you my solemn word."

I had to let the foul pig take a few minor liberties, although I itched to butt him in the face and break his crooked nose for the second time in its life. (The first was at Bosworth, I believe. He got a little bit too close to King Richard.) At last I managed to wriggle free.

When I got home, I sent for Thomas and Rick. I told them about the damage to the park, and my suspicion that the raiders had come from Berkeley's land. I didn't dare mention his attempt on me. I do not exaggerate when I say that my boys would have burned his house about his ears and disembowelled him before the day was an hour older. I didn't want any unpleasantness of that kind. It lowers the tone of the neighbourhood.

"Three Mile Wood is very overgrown, down by the road," I added. "Small wonder that we have outlaws plaguing us. There's plenty of covert. Enough to hide a small army in ambush. Some day, some unfortunate traveller is going to be waylaid, and killed. I can see it coming. I don't know what Berkeley's foresters can be about."

"Berkeley's behind all this trouble, if you ask me," said Thomas. "The stolen cattle. The raid on the park. God knows what else."

"There's no doubt of it," I said. They were taken aback by my certainty, but pleased to have their suspicions confirmed.

"I sure as hell don't like the thought of him marrying my sister," Rick snorted.

"Nor do I. In fact, I'm determined he shall not. But I think he has some hold over your father. A hold that may be difficult to break, unless …'

"Unless he meets with some unfortunate accident," said Thomas.

I nodded. "Quite. He's coming here tomorrow, to pay court to Constance. Completely alone. Let's pray that the outlaws don't hinder his passage."

They exchanged significant glances.

"What time tomorrow?" Rick asked.

"Some time after noon."

Rick grinned. "Careless of him, to ride through the woods without escort," he said.

"Very careless," agreed Thomas, sharpening his dagger on a whetstone. "The pity is that we're all going to be far too busy to ride out to meet him. In fact, we're each and every one of us going to be fully occupied, and some miles away."

Tudor was in no hurry to marry Bessy. He had himself crowned in solitary splendour, and had Parliament declare him our rightful King. The weeks continued to slip by. It was Tudor's way of showing everyone, including Bessy, that he was the man in charge, and that he didn't need Bessy's claim to the throne to shore up his own. (Even though he did.)

If I'd been Bessy, I'd have given him sixty different kinds of hell. But she just kept on being her own, sweet self, and when he did trouble himself to visit her, she always made out that she was delighted to see him. It was the way she had been brought up, I suppose, to be pleasant to whatever fellow fate threw at her.

I was summoned to the presence of the Countess of Richmond. Margaret Beaufort was in her element now that her darling little boy was crowned. It amused her to keep me on my knees for half an hour while she finished reading her book.

"Dame Beauchamp," she said suddenly, just as I was beginning to drift off to sleep, "I deem you a most unfortunate influence on the Lady Elizabeth of York. I think we shall have to consider an alternative location for you. Especially as the Bishop of Rochester informs me that you are not at all inclined to be co-operative."

"How co-operative would you like me to be?" I asked. "I'm ready to say whatever you want me to say. Just give me the script."

"I see. Then perhaps you can begin by informing me of the whereabouts of the Intelligence archives."

I shrugged. "I've rather lost touch, what with one thing and another. I did hear that Lovel destroyed many of them. Why don't you ask him?"

"Lovel is in hiding in Flanders, as you well know."

I didn't know, in point of fact, but I was grateful for the information.

I shrugged. "Much of it will still be at Nottingham, I imagine, where King Richard left it. Somewhere in the middle of it you will find the letter of resignation I handed in immediately after his coronation. After that I was just one of Queen Anne's waiting-women."

"And it was in that capacity, I suppose, that you accompanied the Vaughan ruffians to Brecon, and fired a lead bullet into Bishop Morton's backside? Do me a favour!"

"I was doing my bit for my King. It was all quite unofficial."

"We did find certain items at Nottingham," she admitted, "but there were many files, of the very greatest importance, that were unaccountably missing. Are you quite sure that Lovel destroyed them all?"

"No. How can I be? What exactly are you looking for? The files on the Princes? I've already told my brother of Rochester all there is to know about them."

She stood up. "I am not in the least interested in those peevish brats! Richard murdered them, and as we do not have either the time or the inclination to take the Tower apart, stone by stone, we shall never be able to recover their bodies. Agreed?"

"Absolutely," I said. "If that's the truth you want established, I'll back you up all the way, and even fill in a few details if you like. I just want my husband out of the Tower, and pardoned, and permission to retire to Horton Beauchamp together."

"You dare to bargain with me?"

"I thought that that was what you wanted. It's a good bargain, after all. I've no further interest in politics, I can assure you. I just ask for a quiet life. As for Roger, if he agrees to give his allegiance to your son, you can be pretty damned certain that he'll keep his word. He believes in the Knightly Code."

She snorted. "I didn't think we had any of those still in stock. Such men are often more dangerous than those who can be bought."

"There is a file," I said, "that might be of some small interest to your ladyship. It relates to King Edward's mistresses. He had three regulars, you'll recall. A merry one – Elizabeth Shore. A wise one. And a pious one. He was always very cagey about the identity of the last two. They were great ladies, and King Edward was a great gentleman. He didn't want to hurt their reputations. Hastings knew the truth, of course. How could he not? He was Edward's closest friend, the King's Chamberlain, and Head of Yorkist Intelligence. He opened a file on each of them, but he was very discreet about it. They were not listed in the index, so they were very, very hard to find. I used to speculate about the identity of the pious one in particular. There are few such ladies at Court, and fewer still with influence. It was only when I found the file that I had my answer, and all became obvious. Why King Edward showed you, and your husband, such extraordinary favour, when he had no cause to trust either of you beyond the length of his arm. No obvious reason, that is."

The colour had drained from her face. She sat there, gripping her rosary so hard that you could almost hear the beads crying out in pain.

"Hastings was a threat to your precious reputation," I went on, "and so you roped him into that foolish conspiracy. It was easy for you, with your links with Elizabeth Woodville and the Shore woman. You were all in the same guild, after all. When Richard took him out for you, it suited you down to the ground. Christ, what fools we were not to realise that it was all a set up! You must have known how Richard would react in a case like that. You as good as murdered Hastings."

"You will have great difficulty in proving it," she said, icily.

"I can prove quite a bit of it, with that file. What Hastings didn't know, he made up. And he had a colourful imagination where women were concerned."

"You will hand the file over to me."

"Certainly I will. For a price."

"You are aware, of course, that I can have you persuaded?"

I laughed. "That won't do you any good. The file isn't in my possession. I've an account with the Medici Bank in Bruges, and they have it in their safe deposit room. They are under strict instructions. If the least harm comes to me, or to my husband, they are to hand it over, at once, to the Duchess Margaret of Burgundy. I'm sure that you wouldn't want that to happen. That lady knows a few tricks when it comes to publicity, and I reckon she'd make good use of the information. Just think of the damage it'd do to your image! The pious, chaste, charitable, learned Countess of Richmond, revealed as a right little raver who used to knock King Edward out of action for a week at a time!"

I could tell that she was not pleased.

"Be careful not to set your price too high," she hissed.

"I've already named it. Roger's freedom, and my own. A full pardon for him. His lands restored. I'm not bothered about a place at Court. You meet such common people there nowadays."

"And how can I be sure that you'll not come back for more?"

"You can't," I said, "but I won't. You see, I don't have anything to lose at the moment. Once my husband is safe, and restored to his lands, I'll go out of my way to make sure that things stay that way. There'll be no mileage in offending you, will there?"

"Indeed there will not," she snapped.

I smiled. "Look, there's no need for hard feelings. The bottom line is that you've won. You're the one whose son is King, after all. As a gesture of my good will, I'll even throw in my copy of the pardon that King Richard granted to your brother-in-law the day before Bosworth. I'm sure William Stanley doesn't want anyone to know that he had second thoughts."

I often wonder what Margaret would have done if she had found out that Bessy had been holding the file, and Will Stanley's pardon, all along. To say nothing of Richard's gold, which not only helped us through a very thin time but enabled us in due course to buy a small manor in Suffolk for my younger sons' eventual benefit.

Anyway, the day after Roger received his pardon, and swore allegiance, I nipped along to Margaret's apartments and handed the package over. She gave the papers a cursory look, just to check I hadn't fobbed her off with Buckingham's household account roll or something, and then thrust them into the fire.

"Get out!" she snapped. "Never dare to show your face at Court again."

Roger had his lands back – although we lost for good the bits we were granted after Buckingham's revolt – but we were so tied up in parchment bonds, recognisances and such like, that if we ever put a single foot out of line we'd be utterly ruined. We are still bound to this day, although the Slimebag has granted us some small relief in return for almost ten years of quietness on our part.

Roger was given special orders concerning me. He was responsible for keeping me confined to Horton Beauchamp.

After nine months of marriage, Bessy produced an heir for Tudor, Prince Arthur. (Tudor is under the delusion that he is descended from King Arthur. I suppose we are all entitled to claim descent from a fictional character of our choice. Even Roger reckons to descend from Guy of Warwick.) I used this as an opportunity to petition Bessy to intercede for me, and she did so, catching Tudor in a good mood. I am now free to go anywhere I like, as long as it is in Gloucestershire.

XV

It is good to have Roger home again, and safe. Good also that he is up at the far end of the park with Guy, supervising repairs. It leaves me free to set this down without the risk of finding him watching over my shoulder.

Berkeley did not come to me that afternoon. Just as well, because it's passing difficult to get blood out of a carpet without leaving a horrible stain. At last, I put my knife down on the dresser and relaxed. Then I called for my horse.

I found him in Three Mile Wood, just within the boundary of his manor. He lay on his back, staring up with sightless eyes. A black arrow had pierced his black heart, and there were four others in a neat circle around it. I took time out to spit on his body before I searched it for the evidence I had told him to bring. I tucked a piece of replacement correspondence inside his shirt, and then rode home, and sent a boy to inform the authorities.

I burned the package I had taken from Berkeley without even bothering to read it. I had no interest in his pathetic attempts at forgery.

The authorities duly descended upon us. The Coroner, sundry Justices, and the Under-sheriff of Gloucestershire. All expecting to be fed and wined, of course.

"It was a remarkable piece of archery that killed Sir Humphrey," said the Under-sheriff, during a brief pause in the filling of his face.

"Never seen such a close grouping of arrows in a corpse," agreed the Coroner. "Like something you see at an archery contest when someone is showing off."

"There are hosts of outlaws hereabouts," I told them. "My husband's park was attacked by the rogues only the other day."

"Your Steward, Guy Archer, used to be quite a man with the bow, didn't he?" asked the Under-sheriff.

"Oh, yes," I agreed. "None better. But that was in the old days. His eyes are so dim that he can scarcely keep his accounts. He's not shot on the professional circuit for a good ten years."

"Perhaps he has trained others in his skills?"

"Indeed he has. All our young men practise their archery regularly, in accordance with statute. There are many able archers on this manor."

"I understand that your daughter was to marry Sir Humphrey? Is that so?"

"It was suggested," I agreed.

"Forgive me, but she seems less than distraught."

Constance was chatting to Geoffrey, smiling for the first time in weeks. It was careless of her.

"Sir," I said briskly, "I don't know how matters stand in your household, but my husband is accustomed to the obedience of his family. My girl will marry where she is bidden. We are not so unreasonable that we expect her to love the man into the bargain."

He dipped his nose into his wine again. (It was my best Gascon, far too good for a petty Tudor hireling.)

"Sir Humphrey was carrying a most interesting letter," he said, "addressed to the pretended Duke of York. Pledging his loyalty to the impostor."

"Ah, yes," I said. "Sir Humphrey mentioned that fellow to me. Parkin Windbreak. Something like that. People with silly names are always traitors. Look at that Lambert Simnel for example …"

"There must be some mistake," Thomas objected. "Sir Humphrey was known to all as the King's loyal man."

"Indeed he was," agreed the Coroner, "which makes his defection all the more shocking."

"You really cannot trust anyone these days," I cried. "My husband always says that we should go back to the basics of the Knightly Code."

"The men who killed Sir Humphrey did the King a great service," said the Under-sheriff. "They'll not just be pardoned, but rewarded. If we can but find them."

"Virtue is its own reward," muttered Harry, looking up from his legal textbook.

"Quite," agreed the Under-sheriff. "It's pleasing to add that the letter specifically urged the wretch, Warbeck, not to approach Sir Roger Beauchamp. On the grounds that Sir Roger's loyalty to King Henry had been tested, and was unshakeable. Not that Berkeley referred to our noble sovereign by his proper title. He described him as 'The obnoxious Tudor Slimebag'."

"Shocking," I said, wiping the gravy from my mouth with my largest napkin. "I really don't know what the world is coming to, with all this disrespect for authority."

A few months have passed. Christmas is behind us, and we have the snows piled up at the back door. The winter parlour is cosy, although all that wainscoting I had installed does tend to make it rather gloomy for those of us who wish to write. Still, we have to be modern, don't we?

Life goes on, and still brings its surprises. Roger has been restored to the Commission of the Peace, for the first time since 1485. There's some talk that he'll be High Sheriff before long. Amazing how things turn out, isn't it?

Another surprise is that Sir William Stanley has been arrested and executed for high treason. He said that he'd not fight Perkin Warbeck if the young man turned out to be King Edward's son, and that was enough to convict him. Sounds a bit thin to me. I suspect there must have been more to it than that.

Roger says that it's better not to know everything. I'm not sure that I like the way he says it. He never has explained exactly what he was doing all those weeks in London.

The biggest surprise of all has been a family matter. On Twelfth Night Geoffrey and Constance walked into the parlour together, knelt in front of Roger, and asked permission to be wed, mumbling some nonsense to the effect that they loved one another.

I was amazed that Roger sat still and heard them out. I was even more amazed when, instead of snatching up the very suitable stick that was to hand, he began to talk to them about terms and conditions.

Geoffrey is to complete his training as a lawyer. He is to establish himself in London, where men of that sort flourish like fat maggots on a corpse. Then, and only then, if they are both still of the same mind, will Roger give his consent.

"Your brain must be softening," I said, when they had run off together, delighted. "The boy's mother was a shepherdess, for Christ's sake. He's got no pedigree, no coat of arms, no lands, nothing."

Roger shook his head. "Such things can be purchased, nowadays," he yawned, stretching himself. "Geoffrey promises well. One day the Archers will be every bit as famous in England as the Beauchamps. I call it getting in on the ground floor."

"The girl is young," I pointed out. "What if she changes her mind?"

"She's still free to do so. I didn't speak of betrothal, did I?"

The very next morning I wrote to Bessy, asking her to find a place for Constance in her household, a request that was granted by return of post. It will do the girl no harm to see the wider world, and learn some better manners. She will also have the chance to meet someone more suitable. (Although there are plenty of unsuitable people around nowadays, even in the Queen's household.)

But if it comes down to it, I suppose it's true that a woman could have a worse son-in-law than Geoffrey. He's a bright boy, and will end up as a judge at the very least. Perhaps we'll be able to buy him a seat in Parliament. Like most lawyers, he's good at talking without saying very much, so he should fit in there well enough. I really will have to do something about his pedigree, though. Possibly we can graft him onto the Nevilles somewhere.

Roger and I have been lazing in the garden. Our new neighbour, Richard Berkeley, Humphrey's cousin, rode over earlier with his only daughter, Philippa, to pay us a friendly visit. She has hazel eyes, and they never left Thomas's face all the time she was here. Rick is quite put out. I have the odd feeling she will be back. I approve of a girl who is sensible enough to pick out an heir at first sight.

"Strange how those outlaws seem to have vanished from the face of the earth," said Roger, scanning the horizon.

"Outlaws?"

"The ones who killed Berkeley." He paused significantly. "I don't suppose, by any remote chance, that you had anything to do with it?"

"Roger! What are you saying?"

"That you know how to defend your own, my love."

I turned my head from him. "Humphrey Berkeley accused you of treason."

"I know. He had good cause."

"You mean that you have really given your support to Perkin Warbeck?" I was shocked. Roger had sworn his allegiance to Tudor, after all, and it was not his style to break his word except in an absolute emergency.

"No, but I gave him cause to believe that I had. He was one of those whose loyalty I was ordered to test."

"You've been working for Henry Tudor?"

"How do you think I got out of the Tower, Alianore?"

I stared at him, aghast. I'd never told him about the deal I'd cut with Margaret Beaufort, and it had never occurred to me that he'd struck one of his own. We'd paid for our freedom twice over! I just stopped short of laughing.

"But what about Lovel?" I asked. "Lovel has been here half a dozen times. You never betrayed him."

"Lovel was a friend. I told them from the first that I wouldn't do the dirt on friends. They accepted it. Shits like Berkeley and William Stanley are in a different class. It's been a pleasure to see them ruined. Though I must admit, I was surprised when Berkeley took the bait. And even more surprised when he told Perkin Warbeck, in writing, of my loyalty to King Henry. Hard to explain, that bit."

"Very hard," I agreed.

"Best not to try," he said.

The End

Also Available from BeWrite Books

www.bewrite.net

Zolin – A Rockin' Good Wizard
by Barry Ireland

Wizards with spelling difficulties, witches with attitude, a raving 60's rock band on a trip to another dimension, a convent full of sex-hungry nuns, randy royalty, dragons on the make, even lumps in the plaster ... and these are only a few of the problems faced by Zolin the bewildered trainee wizard and Ajax the small town carpenter when their dimensiverses collide.

Zany Barry Ireland picks up where the late Douglas Adams left off his blockbusting Hitchhikers Guide to the Galaxy series, and throws improbability into overdrive.

A rare Laugh Out Loud book which might be embarrassing to read in the company of strangers in a railway carriage or to remember at board meetings and funerals.

Ireland's hilariously peopled worlds are dangerous to the health of tummy muscles and funny bones.

'A little gem' The Sunday Express.
Paperback ISBN 1-904224-19-9

The Kinnons of Candleriggs
by Jenny Telfer Chaplin

An uncompromising story of one woman's life in Victorian Glasgow.

Kate, a chamber maid, pregnant and unexpectedly married to the son of Irish landed gentry, expects a life fitting her husband's status, but her husband is cut off without a penny by his family. So, instead, as poverty-stricken Irish immigrants considered the lowest of the low by the Glaswegians, she has to battle religious, cultural, and social prejudice.

Told with humour, compassion, and a keen insight into the period, this is a first rate read.
Paperback ISBN 1-904492-94-9

Ring of Stone
by Hugh McCracken

Two groups of teenagers – one middle-class students struggling for social justice, the other bar room toughs out for a brawl to right their own perceived wrongs – are thrust through a twist in the loop of time to the violent days of Medieval England.

Trapped in a dark era where human life is cheaper than bread and horrific torture is a popular entertainment, they find they must join forces or die.

Dogged by death every step of the way, each finds that experience of modern life has provided a skill that might – just might – save the band from an excruciating fate. And one of the group – having lost a brother to the barbaric torture death of impaling – hides a very special secret.

But as well as their own struggle for survival, the youngsters – each a convinced protestor – find themselves in a moral dilemma ... how to save their own skins whilst also fighting against the inhuman brutality and injustice suffered by new friends in a time where they don't belong.

In the latest in his popular Time Shift series, Hugh McCracken transports his readers into the harsh realities of days gone by with a unique talent for interweaving breathtaking adventure and fine historical detail.

These utterly believable pages turn faster and faster to reach an unforgettable climax as McCracken casts his spell.
Paperback ISBN 1-904224-61-X

Treason
by Meredith Whitford

Treachery in Love and War in the Struggle for the English Crown

From the time he sees his parents brutally slain and his home destroyed in a bloody Lancastrian power struggle for the crown, young Martin Robsart's life becomes entwined with that of England's royal Plantagenet family.

Through the turbulence of civil war, Martin serves his cousins - Yorkist kings Edward IV and Richard III - and learns the cost of loyalty and love in battlefields and bedchambers in a time when life is cheap and treachery hides behind a smile.

Through Martin's eyes, Meredith Whitford's superbly researched and richly woven novel shows Shakespeare's conniving and perverse Richard III in a realistic new light - as a patriot and a lover.

Never before has perceived history taken such a surprising turn as Whitford corrects the Shakespearean myth and crowns a new hero, bringing back to life the passion and heat of a breathless historical moment that shaped the world - a moment we know as the War of the Roses ...a time of thorns and treason.
Paperback ISBN 1-904492-72-X

The Stones of Petronicus
by Peter Tomlinson

A new-born baby is left naked and exposed to die on a city wall while his father is hanged for petty theft a few feet away amid the cheers and hoots of a crazed mob.

Petronicus, an itinerant healer and man of wisdom, takes the babe to heart and together they begin a quest for knowledge, groping through a maze of magic and madness to find answers in the cruel and mysterious ancient world.

The boy grows to manhood in strange lands where a chosen few risk death in their search for truth, bitterly opposed by ruthless rulers and puppet priests who strive to enslave their subjects in a perpetual Dark Age of superstition and suspicion.

The heart-warming, honest but complex simplicity Petronicus and his adopted son share leave the reader wiser than when he joined them on their remarkable journey.

Not since the Fables of Aesop has a book like this been written. And Tomlinson wraps the sage advices in the tales Petronicus tells in a story as intriguing and exciting as any high-octane thriller - with characters so real you'll meet them time and again in your dreams ... and your nightmares.
Paperback ISBN 1-904492-76-2

Jahred and The Magi
by Wilma Clark

Set against the exotic cities and cruel times of the Middle East two thousand years ago, this is a story of bitter intrigue and dangerous honesty, valour and cowardice, love and hate, death ... and birth.

Jahred, his father imprisoned for outspoken prophecies, grows to young manhood in kingdoms of the wise and the wicked where one flattering remark can earn the favour of princes and one wrong word can bring torture and death.

Jahred – wise beyond his years – is charged with a quest to prove his father's prophecy true. On his journey, he joins with others – the famous Magi of Christian tradition – making the same quest for reasons of their own ... following the strange star they believe will lead them to a King who will rule over all kings.

A fast-paced thriller of a novel, superbly researched and intelligently told, which explains in realistic, unsentimental words who the mysterious Three Wise Men, who make only a brief appearance in the New Testament, might have been.
Paperback ISBN 1-904224-76-8

Crime

The Knotted Cord	Alistair Kinnon
The Tangled Skein	Alistair Kinnon
Marks	Sam Smith
Porlock Counterpoint	Sam Smith
Scent of Crime	Linda Stone
The End of Science Fiction	Sam Smith

Crime/Humour

Sweet Molly Maguire	Terry Houston

Fantasy/Humour

The Hundredfold Problem	John Grant
Earthdoom!	David Langford & John Grant

Collections/ Short Stories

As the Crow Flies	Dave Hutchinson
The Loss of Innocence	Jay Mandal
Kaleidoscope	Various
Odie Dodie	Lad Moore
Tailwind	Lad Moore
The Miller Moth	Mike Broemmel
The Shadow Cast	Mike Broemmel
As the Crow Flies	Dave Hutchinson
The Creature in the Rose	Various

General

The Wounded Stone	Terry Houston
Magpies and Sunsets	Neil Alexander Marr
Redemption of Quapaw Mountain	Bertha Sutliff

Romance

A Different Kind of Love	Jay Mandal
The Dandelion Clock	Jay Mandal

Humour

The Cuckoos of Batch Magna	Peter Maughan

Adventure

Matabele Gold	Michael J Hunt
The African Journals of Petros Amm	Michael J Hunt

All the above titles are available from

www.bewrite.net

Printed in the United States
214322BV00001B/9/A

9 781904 492788